D0216666

SUICIDE

Scholars Press
Studies in the Humanities Series

Number 1
John Donne
SUICIDE

Biathanatos transcribed and edited for modern readers
by William A. Clebsch
Stanford University

John Donne
SUICIDE

Biathanatos transcribed and edited for modern readers

by William A. Clebsch
Stanford University

Scholars Press
Chico, California

Library of Congress Cataloging in Publication Data

Donne, John, 1572–1631.
  Suicide : biathanatos.

  (Scholars Press studies in the humanities series ; no. 1)
  1. Suicide—Early works to 1800. I. Clebsch, William A.
II. Title. III. Series.
HV6544.D7 1983   362.2   83–4466
ISBN 0-89130-623-4
ISBN 0-89130-624-2 (pbk.)

Printed in the United States of America

CONTENTS

EDITOR'S INTRODUCTION

William A. Clebsch

Every human society whose members' behavior is detailed in extant records has included individuals who by their own decision and agency forfeited their own lives. Depending on the circumstances of their deaths, their fellows either memorialized them as heroes or condemned them as misguided or weak or evil persons. For most of their histories the Western societies that the Christian religion shaped have condemned suicides. It was not so in the first few Christian centuries, but since the deed of self-murder became a major sin—and right down to modern times—few indeed have been the writers who espoused Christianity and applauded or even excused suicide. Of these few, the writing that makes up this book is one of the earliest and most profound.

Poets and historians no less than philosophers and priests have shown extraordinary fascination with this form of human death, naming it by such varied terms as self-murder, cowardice, the supreme sacrifice, martyrdom, or suicide. For Aristotle it represented unmitigated cowardice—more technically, pusillanimity—yet many of the Roman writers who revered him regarded it as courageous. For Jesus it represented, when done for the sake of a friend, that love than which there could be no greater, yet the Christians who worshipped him came to condemn it as one of the very few sins lying beyond the reach of God's forgiveness.

In Asian societies the deed has tended to be noncontroversial and rather honorable than despicable. Yet even for modern Westerners given to relativistic ethics it remains unsettling and perplexing, even as its acknowledged practice becomes increasingly widespread and its moral justifications more and more persuasive. In the latter societies the living who are not contemplating how to bring about their own ends find it difficult to regard suicide as capable of rational explanation. Quite possibly suicide is the aspect of individual behavior presenting the greatest difficulty of mutual understandings between the Oriental and the Occidental forms of humanity.

To the very heart of this Western perplexity about suicide as absurd the ensuing pages probe, wrestling with the stark fact that, when successful, the act of intentionally dying by one's own agency defies first-hand testimony. Among the things that people intentionally do, this one is unique in that in the nature of the case nobody can tell us what it was like to have done it. Stoics and samurai no less than soldiers and Christian martyrs have done it resolutely, confident that it was the honorable course that led to a good name on earth and to the best reward wherever the souls of the departed may go. Yet since Christianity gained recognition as a legal religion it has damned the memory of suicides here and consigned their souls to perdition hereafter. In that respect Christianity among the world religions is unique, and so far as that attitude permeated Western culture it made that culture unique.

The Christian religion originated in an act of willing acceptance of death, and its earliest exemplars were persons who imitated that act for the sake of their faith. The religion's savior refused to do anything when, by all accounts, he could easily have done enough, to avoid dying. By lending his agency to his own death, again by all accounts, he atoned for his followers' sins. Ironically, by later Christian doctrine this act became a sin for which his similar act could not atone.

The religion won success in the pagan culture in which it found itself, according to the unanimous conviction of its most influential thinkers, by martyrdom—an act in which persons behaved in such a way as to bring about their own deaths. "The blood of the martyrs," wrote Tertullian in North Africa at the beginning of the third century, "is the seed of the church."[1] No Christian whose writings are preserved to us disagreed with him. According to his teaching, only these martyrs—if the intention be tantamount to the act then only these suicides—gained immediate entry into heaven. No known writer of the early church disagreed with this regard for the martyrs. Only they had direct access to and influence over the heavenly dispensers of mercies and favors to earthly believers. Their graves were the sites for especially solemn religious celebrations and the scenes for extraordinary miracles, and many of them remain so today for the faithful.

When the monks displaced the martyrs as the model Christians, hard upon the accommodation of the Empire and the Church, these special spiritual privileges were also transferred. In the phrase used by Saint Athanasius to describe the life of Saint Antony, a prototypical desert monk, "he was a martyr every day" through self-inflicted austerities.[2] Later on, Christian mystics achieved symbolic termination of moral, bodily, earthly living by transitory union with the savior in heaven, and they studied hard to do so by their own agency—assisted, of course, by divine grace.

If it seems harsh to call Jesus, the martyrs, the monks, and the mystics Christian suicides, then the intention is not tantamount to the act, for many surely intended their own deaths. In that case, call them not self-killing persons but only self-dying persons. But as the pages of this book unfold, be

---

[1] *Apology*, chap. 50.
[2] *Life of Antony*, chap. 47.

prepared to defend the separation of intention from action and to find a way to classify these persons other than as self-murderers—in Donne's preferred term, "self-homicides." (The word "suicide" entered the English language long after the book was composed.)

Donne called his book by a term representing slightly garbled Greek—*Biathanatos*, which means to die violently. He used for what moderns call suicide the term "self-homicide," and he did so repeatedly, thereby heightening the paradoxical character of the very concept he was discussing, since homicide denotes causing another's death. Keeping up with Donne's plays on language shortly becomes demanding; it is a concession to his mastery that this edition is called by the simple, current, ambiguous term *Suicide*. Many other terms commonly used in Donne's day have been changed to our equivalent (if debased and inflated) coinage; why not also his title? On every page of this edition has arisen the perplexity that every translator faces, that to keep a thought one has to change a word. So be it with *Biathanatos* rendered *Suicide*.

Whatever one calls the savior and his model disciples for having willed their own deaths, the categorical condemnation of willing one's own death in traditional Christianity arose from a sea-change in attitude toward suicide. Writing about a century after the Roman Empire and the Christian Church joined forces with one another, Saint Augustine of Hippo formulated what became the traditional Christian condemnation of suicide. His explicit grounds were simple. The commandment of Yahweh, "You shall not kill," applied universally.[3] Of course, there were approved exceptions in the tradition, the most notable of whom was Samson, who pulled down the pillars of the Philistines' hall to crush them—and himself. By Augustine's time Samson was revered as a type of Christ, precisely for his fidelity to God even unto death. His case Augustine excused on the one basis for which he made suicide allowable—direct and particular orders from God.

The pages of this book show that it is no easier to demonstrate that every approved Christian suicide had such orders than it is to argue persuasively that suicide is unforgiveable because no suicide could repent of his or her act. The book takes as strong a stand against Augustine's condemnation of the deed as it does against his sole exception. It does not, however, press its case against Augustine by pointing out that his implicit reasons for condemning suicide were rooted more profoundly in his commitment to neo-Platonic philosophy than in his commitment to Christian theology. From the former viewpoint, willing self-destruction was particularly disagreeable because it required the self-contradictory disposition of self-hate, which defied the human soul's derivation from and participation in the world-soul.

3 Exodus 20:13.

The new classification of suicide as an act of murder placed it among the three sins that the early church regarded as truly unredeemable. (The others were adultery, which referred to any gross sexual irregularity, and apostasy or repudiation of one's status as a Christian.) Put another way, Augustine saw to it that he assigned suicide to the gravest class of sins. The martyrs had already become legendary heroes and heroines when Augustine lived and wrote. In fact, the fourth-century Christian historian, Eusebius Pamphili, had built his ecclesiastical history around tales of the martyrs as Christians whose souls were made immortal by their deaths—occasions which, as Donne points out, had been called their "heavenly birthdays." In short, they were regarded as divinized Christians, and of course that regard carried the clear implication that whatever they did as they died was done under special divine guidance or inspiration. Thus Augustine could as it were have his cake and eat it too by condemning suicide and retaining regard for the martyrs as persons who died as they did at the particular behest of the deity. By lights, then, there was much to be gained and nothing to be lost by interpreting the commandment as meaning, "You shall not kill, and in no case shall you kill yourself unless God patently calls you to do so."

From Augustine down the centuries to the time of the Reformation this doctrine stood unchallenged in Latin theology. Saint Thomas Aquinas accepted it and undergirded it by elevating self-preservation to the status of a universal natural law. The most powerful argument against Augustine and Aquinas on suicide to flow from the pen of a Christian moral theologian is the argument spelled out in this book. If it was not the very first, it surely was the first for a very long time, to attempt a reversal of the reversal that Augustine had initiated.

John Donne, English poet and preacher, stood squarely within the bounds of Christian doctrine and piety in setting forth this audacious and fascinating argument. He pleaded that the blanket condemnation of suicide sprang from a lack of charity toward the neighbor. It presumed more than it could know in declaring that suicides could not repent. It shackled God's grace in declaring suicide a sin for which there could be no remission. It blinded itself to a profound and universal human yearning for death that was demonstrable from personal experience and historical records.

All these arguments Donne framed into three parts of his book, the first on natural law, the second on positive law, the third on divine law. That framing was traditionally accepted without objections to the repetitions and postponements that it necessitated. But despite these flaws—which is what they are if the argument is evaluated from the standpoint of modern, post-Ramus logic—Donne's case against condemning suicide outright shows a remarkable consistency and integrity. For example, the fact that he detected within his own person—as well as within the history of humanity far and wide in time and space—a deep yearning for death challenged Aquinas's widely accepted principle that self-preservation was a universal law of nature. At the same time, Donne's attention to the human urge to die exhibits empathy with a long list of suicides who had been damned on the Augustinian–Aquinian principles, and that empathy undergirds the argument that in Christian charity moral theologians should be slow to condemn and fast to defend human actions. Further, Donne's argument that the act of suicide neither demonstrably precluded repentance by its doer nor put his soul beyond the reach of God's forgiveness became a double-edged sword, sharpened on one side by the hard rationality that moral theologians practiced and on the other by the piety they professed.

Donne in his own right was an accomplished moral theologian, and to that endeavor he brought formal legal training. He knew the pagan classics as well as the church Fathers, civil law as well as canon law, and he brought to the genre of moral theology a rare flair for rhetoric and humor.

By Donne's time the disputes in Western Europe over moral actions that carried religious sanctions had developed into a formal and specialized literary genre. English moral theology in his day—the late sixteenth and early seventeenth centuries—had gone far beyond the yes-and-no rhythms by which scholastic disputations embraced within the writer's conclusions both some apparently contradictory views (by means of subtly altering them) and some actual contradictions (by means of refuting or ridiculing them). The early medieval mode of citing, arranging, and commenting upon sentences drawn from accepted or authoritative writers had long since been combined with and employed in dialectical disputation. On its face, *Biathanatos* belongs to the later medieval genre, exemplified perhaps at its best by Aquinas's *Summa Theologica*.

But Donne in point of fact had mastered the techniques of arranging sentences and of dialectical disputation so thoroughly that he readily went beyond them, so that under its surface *Biathanatos* is a far more subtle work than the old genre could contain. In a word, it is medieval moral theology at the hands of a distinctly Renaissance author; it exhibits Donne's own wits and his own wit as well.

Compared with other writings of moral theology by Renaissance Englishmen, this work is distinctive in that the author's personality and personal sensibilities shine through even the duller sections. That is not true, for example, of William Ames's *Marrow of Divinity*, which first appeared less than two decades after *Biathanatos*. This treatise, a favorite of the Puritans, presented a more comprehensive and a more dogmatic tendency toward principles so grand as to make it frequently difficult for the modern reader to relate them to concrete problems of behavior. Nor is it true, by contrast, of Jeremy Taylor's *Ductor Dubitantium* (1660), a favorite of the Anglicans. The latter stands for the modern reader so mired in specific—albeit fictional—aspects of behavior that it is difficult to relate the details to moral principles.

Donne accurately described his approach and the ways in which it differs from that of Ames and that of Taylor in a pithy sentence: "Morall Divinity becomes us all; but Naturall Divinity, and Metaphysic Divinity, almost all may spare."[4] In these terms, although Ames and Taylor were writing what is commonly called moral theology, Ames's verged on the metaphysic and Taylor's veered toward the natural.

With the carving of Europe just after the Reformation into territories in which all subjects had to conform to their rulers' religions, whether the ruler changed religions or a change in rulers changed the religion, Christian religiousness found twin common denominators in moralism and pietism; only the former is of interest here.[5] Then Protestants no less than Catholics drew upon Aquinas's moral theology, a combination of Aristotelian and Christian ethics, and everybody tuned the harp of the Angelic Doctor to his own version of Christianity and to his own political and social circumstances. Dominican scholars, with their birthright claim on Aquinas, emphasized the conscience as seeking probable sanctions for behavior, and among probabilities there might be choices. Jesuits on the whole sought to expand personal liberty to its farthest permissible limits, so long as the moral law's letter could be bent to individual circumstances without breaking. Calvinists and in England Puritans enthroned scripture as the norm, whether by precept or precedent, for what godly men and women might do in this life to assure their bliss in the life to come. Anglicans justified moral action by appealing to scripture, reason, and tradition. Only the Lutherans who literalized their principle of justification by faith alone and not by works tended to eschew this otherwise pervasive moralism—not the opposite but the accompaniment to pietism. Cases of conscience, that is to say, by Donne's time were becoming the key to as well as the content of Christian theology in the West, reconceived as the study of God's will for creatures made in his image and Christ's will for followers baptized into his redemption.

The study of cases of conscience, widely known as casuistry, impressed Donne rather less than it impressed most moral theologians of his age. Otherwise, his book ran the gamut of those theologians' concerns—natural

---

[4] John Donne, *Essays in Divinity*, ed. Evelyn M. Simpson (Oxford: Clarendon, 1952), p. 88; the passage was cited by Henry R. McAdoo, *The Structure of Caroline Moral Theology* (London: Longman's, Green, 1949), p. 13n., from the edition by Augustus Jessopp (London: John Tupling, 1855), p. 218 and mistakenly attributed to p. 219; McAdoo in this work referred frequently to Donne as a Caroline moral theologian, but made no mention of *Biathanatos*.

[5] See William A. Clebsch, *Christianity in European History* (New York: Oxford University Press, 1977), chap. 5.

law, positive law, divine law. He argued, like the good Anglican that he was not yet, from the authority of the church Fathers as well as from scripture, and the reasoning by which he argued was itself a source of religious authority. Like the good Catholic that he had not yet stopped being, he lodged his reasoning in the debates of Dominican and Franciscan and Jesuit casuists and canonists. True to both of these roles, he took seriously canon law as it had been shaped throughout the history of the church. He cited as his sources Protestants like Beza and Calvin as well as Catholics like Neri and Toledo, Englishmen as well as Continentals, jurists as well as theologians. Principles, however, interested him more than examples, and in that he was his own thinker.

Although Donne confessed at the beginning of his book that he had often, and not morbidly, considered taking his own life, and although he thought it more charitable to look for good motives in the acts of others than for bad, he was careful not to counsel others to die by their own willing hands. Nor can there be any suspicion that he himself eventually died that way. Still, as his poems and sermons as well as this book attest, he regarded death as a potential friend and not as in inevitable enemy. The sculptor Nicholas Stone carved the monument to Donne, a statue still to be seen in Saint Paul's Cathedral in London. For the work Donne "sat," standing in his study before a fire, his eyes shut, his winding-sheet wrapped and tied around him, his feet resting upon a funeral urn. Still, "It is believed that his [terminal] disease," in the phrase of the eleventh edition of the Britannica, "was a malarial form of recurrent quinsy acting upon an extremely neurotic system"—quinsy being what later parlance calls tonsilitis.[6]

It honors Donne's own preoccupation to introduce by mention of his death a brief summary of his life. The main thing to note is that he wrote this book at a low point, financially strapped, uncertain as to vocation, religiously in transition. None of those circumstances indicates any unseriousness about his topic. Nor is the fact that he checked his original intention to publish the work an indication that he retracted any part of the argument, for he took care that it should be not destroyed but preserved—if not published, certainly not burned.

Born in London either late in 1571 or early in 1572, Donne lived most of his life in that city and for the last decade was Dean of its diocesan Cathedral. There his father, who had prospered in trade, had died when John was a young boy. There his mother lived as a member of the most prominent Roman Catholic families in the land, at a time when that religion's adherents were oppressed under the conformist religious policies of Queen Elizabeth I. Donne was precise when he wrote in the preface to this book, "I had my first breeding and conversation with men

[6] VIII, 418c.

of a suppressed and afflicted religion, accustomed to despising death and hungry for an imagined martyrdom."

That conversation—not, of course, the literal breeding—was mainly among Jesuits, who educated him and spearheaded the pope's campaign to regain the allegiance of Englishmen. His uncle had directed the Jesuits' missionary work in England until he was arrested, and after seventeen years in prison he was exiled from his native land. Donne's brother, arrested for concealing in his room a priest of the Roman Catholic Church (likely a Jesuit), contracted in prison a fatal fever. Donne's own university studies, first at Oxford and then at Cambridge, led to no academic degrees because an oath of allegiance to the Church of England was required at graduation. He studied law in London and read romance literature. From London and back again he traveled in Italy and Spain. In London he investigated points at issue between his family's Church and his country's Church, as his dissatisfaction with the former turned slowly into adherence to the latter.

Donne became secretary for four years at the turn of the century to Sir Thomas Egerton, lord keeper of the Great Seal, whose niece and protégée, Ann More, he secretly married. Ann's father, enraged, tried to annul or wreck the marriage. For his wife and "three gamesome children"—there would eventually be a dozen, of whom seven lived beyond infancy—Donne eked out a living doing scholarly chores.[7] A major one consisted of studying the church Fathers on points of dispute between Anglicans and Roman Catholics for his friend Thomas Morton, who in 1607 became Dean of Gloucester. Morton offered Donne an ecclesiastical position if he would become ordained, but in conscience he could not do so for the sake of worldly gain rather than at the calling of God. Under these circumstances of material insecurity, personal unrest, and mental anguish he wrote *Biathanatos*. To the year 1608 its composition may confidently be ascribed.

Donne had contemplated not only suicide, which he admits freely in this book, but also emigrating to Virginia in the early years of what became that colony's enduring establishment. From such steps he was saved, if saving he needed, by his father-in-law's change of heart. Belated payment of the marriage dowry enabled Donne to embark upon a literary career. Perhaps it was this turn of fortune that relieved him from publishing *Biathanatos*, a step he had intended but foreswore after friends at both universities advised that the work contained a certain false thread of argumentation that almost defied detection. Only that much do his records tell us; surely those friends recognized that the book falsified a long-revered tradition of condemning suicide on Christian grounds, but their false thread remains untraced.

[7] *Letters*, cited by Evelyn M. Simpson, *A Study of the Prose Works of John Donne*, 2d ed. (Oxford: Clarendon, 1948), p. 22, n. 1.

By 1610 he was publishing a work designed to persuade Roman Catholics to declare political allegiance to King James I. The next year, during which that king's authorized version of the Bible was published, he wrote an open attack on the Jesuits. By then he assuredly subscribed to the Church of England, but his interests still inclined more to a political than to an ecclesiastical career. His talents, regardless of professional interest, were making him into a poet. Meanwhile, the king was more easily persuaded to advance him as a minister of the Church than as a minister of State. In January 1615 he was ordained. Two years later, his wife died, and grief began to permeate his poems and sermons. By 1621 he was Dean of Saint Paul's, and office he held until his death in 1631.

The fact that the first publication of the book only came about sixteen years after the author's death has been interpreted by most—and the most reliable—students of the work as in no way qualifying the arguments and convictions set forth in it. Donne wrote it intending to publish it himself, as is clear from the preface. "I present and expose it to all who have candor and neutrality," he declared, "in order to escape the just reproof of Jerome, 'A new kind of malice and intemperance is to communicate what you wish to hide.'" (Nor was Donne communicating clandestinely by citing Jerome in Latin!) "I wish," he continued, "and, as much as I can, bring it about that to those many learned and subtle men who have traveled over this point, some charitable and compassionate men might be added." These aims, then, stand firm and clear in Donne's own words, which he did not erase even when he decided not to have the book printed.

For the basis of that decision only surmises are available, and none so far advanced is entirely convincing. Surely he was influenced by the fact that friends in the universities advised against publication. He wrote about paradoxes, he called suicide or self-homicide a paradox, and he pardoxically directed those to whom he sent the manuscript that it should neither be published nor destroyed. He also noted that it had been written by him before he became the well-known clergyman that he later was—by Jack Donne, not Dr. Donne.

The paradox became resolved when the son decided, during the early years of Puritan ascendancy in England, that the only way he could avoid the work's destruction was by publishing it. So he did. It may be legitimate to surmise that the son would have best understood his deceased father's intentions, but the notion carries no more weight than surmises ought to carry. It remains a plain fact, however, that in deciding to publish the work the son was carrying out the initial and plain, if not the later and paradoxical, intention of the father.

These and other details about the manuscript and its printings are to be found in scholarly editions of *Biathanatos*, and they need not detain us in this modern reader's edition. In sum, the first printing of 1647 was reissued twice, first in 1700 with minor emendations and again in 1930 as a facsimile of the 1647 printing.

Interest in Donne's book has broadened among scholars since the late 1960s. Charles Thomas Mark in 1970 won his doctoral degree at Princeton University with a dissertation entitled, "John Donne: *Biathanatos*. A Critical Edition with Introduction and Commentary." In 1973 Ernest Walter Sullivan II won that degree at the University of California in Los Angeles with "A Critical, Old-Spelling Edition of John Donne's *Biathanatos*." More recently, *Biathanatos: A Modern-Spelling Edition, with Introduction and Commentary*, by Michael Rudick and M. Pabst Battin, Garland English Texts, Number 1 (New York and London: Garland Publishing) became available in 1982. In the same year the University of Delaware Press announced an edition by Dr. Sullivan, to be published also in London by Associated University Presses. As the edition in hand was going to press, Dr. Sullivan wrote that he expected publication in May 1983. Like his dissertation, this edition will retain old spelling and will include extensive scholarly paraphernalia. Through correspondence with editors at Oxford University Press I learned that yet another scholarly edition was being prepared for publication by Dr. Mark and Helen Peters. I put forth this reader's edition, of course, for a use that I am reluctant to call nonscholarly but that is not scholarly in just the way that the abovementioned editions are.

When this reader's edition was nearly complete, the editor was able to examine the rich introduction and commentary provided by Rudick and Battin. Where I have learned from their tracings of Donne's sources, credit is given in the glossary. I have not referenced the several instances at which their translations from the Latin or from earlier English prompted me to reconsider those that I had made; these were not many, and many reconsiderations led me to prefer my renderings over theirs. For example, in rendering Donne's "*recta ratio*," commonly and by Rudick and Battin Englished as "right reason," I have preferred the more cumbersome "rectified reason"—not for the sake of being disagreeable or antiquarian but simply because where Donne himself expressed this phrase in English he preferred "rectified reason" and because I therefore deem that the participial modifier more closely conveys his meaning. On similar grounds, I have translated "*sui juris*" not "his own judge" nor even "a law unto himself" but "judge in his own cause."

The first printed edition of the book was divided into Parts, Distinctions, Sections, and topics; this edition keeps all but the last, numbering paragraphs that begin new sections. By these clues readers may find their places in the facsimile edition or one of the recent scholarly editions. The first printing also included a long "distribution of the work" into these divisions—a kind of elaborate table of contents the reproduction of which in this edition seemed at best unnecessary and at worst distracting. Donne put his "footnotes" referring to the sources he cited in the margins; here they are elided, since Rudick and Battin reproduce them with comments and corrections. To the original Donne appended a list of authors he quoted, roughly in the order of their appearance. Replacing that list in this edition is an alphabetical glossary of proper names, with a brief identification of each and with page-references to the text—a kind of indexed prosopography of Donne's sources. The reader who is unfamiliar with these authorities can meet them in this way, and the more expert reader can learn from the glossary what broad scholarly erudition undergirds Donne's argument that the traditional Christian condemnation of suicides is, in a word, un-Christian.

A number of colleagues at Stanford have generously assisted me in various particulars. Professor Hester Gelber (Religious Studies) helped with some of Donne's Latin citations. The following helped me track down certain persons whom Donne cited: Professors Lawrence V. Berman and Edwin M. Good (Religious Studies); Edward Courtney, John Winkler, and Marsh H. McCall, Jr. (Classics); and Messrs. Ira Levine and James Knox (Green Library). I end with the usual disclaimer that their involvement implicates them in none of my errors.

Debra Skriba, team-teacher par excellence, and the honors students who have explored with us human predicaments like servitude, rebellion, and suicide, more than earned the dedication to them in gratitude of my work on this edition. To the generous and anonymous founder of the George Edwin Burnell Professorship of Religious Studies at Stanford, which I am privileged to hold, I owe and hereby tender very special thanks.

Stanford University   *March 1983*

BIATHANATOS

A Declaration of the Paradox or Thesis that Self-homicide is not so Naturally a Sin that it May Never Be Otherwise;

in which the nature and the extent of all the laws which seem to be violated by this act are diligently surveyed.

Written by John Donne, who afterwards was ordained in the Church of England and died Dean of Saint Paul's, London. . . .

"I do not profess everything to be true. But I will roil the waters for the readers' profit."

Published by Authority.
London.
Printed for John Dawson.

THE EPISTLE DEDICATORY

To the right honorable Lord Philip Herbert: My lord, although I have not exactly obeyed your commands, yet I hope I have exceeded them by presenting to your honor this treatise, which is so much the better for being none of my own and which perchance may deserve to live for facilitating the issues of death.

It was written long since by my father and by him forbidden both the press and the fire; neither would I have subjected it now to the public view. But I could find no certain way to defend it from the one save by committing it to the other. For since the beginning of this war, my study having been often searched and all my books (almost my brains) by their continual alarums sequestered for the use of the Committee, two dangers appeared more eminently to hover over this work, being then a manuscript—the danger of being utterly lost and the danger of being utterly found. These dangers are fathered by some of those wild atheists who, as if they came into the world by conquest, own all other men's wits and are resolved to be learned, in spite of their stars, which would fairly have inclined them to a more modest and honest course of life.

Your lordship's protection will defend this innocent writing from these two monsters, men who cannot write and men who cannot read, and I am very confident that all those who can will think it may deserve this favor from your lordship. For although this book appears under the form of a paradox, still I desire your lordship to look upon this doctrine as a firm and established truth.

"To dare death gives life."

Your lordship's most humble servant,
John Donne   From my house in Covent Garden 28.

AUTHORS CITED IN THIS BOOK

[Donne listed his sources roughly in the order of their citation; for their names, dates, and identifications, arranged alphabetically, consult this edition's Glossary of Names.]

In citing these authors, for those whom I produce only for ornament and illustration I have trusted my own old notes; although I have no reason to suspect them, still I here confess my laziness in that I did not refresh them by going to the original. Of those few whom I have not seen in the original books themselves (for there are some such, even of texts cited for the greatest force), besides the integrity of my purpose, I have this safe defense against any quarreler: whatever text I cite from any Catholic author, if I have not considered the book itself, then I cite him from another Catholic writer, and the same course I hold with the Protestants. So I shall hardly be condemned for any false citation, unless to make me an accessory they pronounce one of their own friends the prinicipal.

THE PREFACE

*Declaring the Reasons, the Purpose,
the Way, and the End of the Author*

Beza, a man as eminent and illustrious in the full glory and noon of learning as others were in the dawning and morning (when even the least sparkle was notorious) confesses of himself that but for the anguish of a running sore on his head, he would have drowned himself from the Miller's Bridge in Paris, if his uncle just then had not by chance come that way. I often have such a sickly inclination. Whether it is because I had my first breeding and conversation with men of a suppressed and afflicted religion, accustomed to despising death and hungry for an imagined martyrdom; or because the common enemy finds that door in me worst locked against him; or because there is a perplexity and flexibility in the doctrine itself; or because my conscience always assures me that no rebellious grudging at God's gifts or other sinful concurrence accompanies these thoughts in me; or because a brave scorn or a faint cowardliness beget it whenever any affliction assails me—whatever the reason, I think I have the keys of my prison in my own hand, and no remedy presents itself so quickly to my heart as my own sword. Often, meditation on this act has won me to a charitable interpretation of their action who die thus and has provoked me a little to watch and attack the reasons of those who pronounce such peremptory judgments upon them.

A devout and godly man has guided us well and rectified our uncharitableness in such cases by this remembrance, "You know this man's fall, but you do not know his wrestling, which perhaps was such that his fall itself is almost justified and accepted by God." For to this end, says Bosquier, "God has appointed us temptations that we might have some excuses for our sins when he calls us to account." It is an uncharitable misinterpreter who unthriftily demolishes his own house and does not repair another; he loses without any gain or profit to anybody. Tertullian, comparing and making equal one who provokes another and one who will be provoked by another, says, "There is no difference, but that the provoker offended first, and that is nothing, because in evil there is no respect of order or priority." So we may quickly become as evil as any offender, if we offend by severely reproving his act. For John Climacus in his *Ladder of Paradise* places these two steps very near to one another when he says, "Although in the world it would be possible for you to escape all defiling by actual sin, yet by your judging and condemning those who are defiled you are defiled." Basil notes that you are defiled because "In comparing others' sins you cannot avoid excusing your own." Especially this is done if your zeal is too fervent in reprehending others. For as in most other happenings, so in this one also, sin has the nature of poison, in that "It enters the easiest and works the fastest upon choleric constitutions." It is a good counsel of the Pharisees, "Do not judge a neighbor before you stand in his place." "Feel and wrestle with such temptations as he has done, and your zeal will be tamer." "Therefore," says the apostle, "it was fitting for Christ to be like us, so that he might be merciful" (Hebr. 2:10).

After a Christian affirmation of an innocent purpose, after submitting all that is said not only to every Christian church but to every Christian man, and after an entreaty that the reader will follow this advice of Judah ben Tabbai, "May those who quarrel be in your sight both bad and guilty," and that the reader will trust neither me nor the adverse party but the reasons—if then there is any scandal in this enterprise of mine, it is taken, not given. I know that malicious, prejudiced men and lazy affecters of ignorance will use the same calumnies and protests toward me, for the voice and sound of the snake and goose is all one. Nevertheless, because I thought that, as in the pool of Bethsaida there was no healing till the water was troubled (John 5:2–9), so the best way to find the truth in this matter is to debate and examine it. "We must dispute about truth as well as for truth," wrote Athenagoras. Thus I did not for fear of misinterpretation abstain from this undertaking. Our stomachs now are not so tender and queasy, after feeding so long upon solid divinity, nor are we so suspicious and afraid, having been so long enlightened in God's path, that we should think any truth strange to us or relapse into that childish age in which a council in France forbade Aristotle's *Metaphysics* and punished with excommunication either the copying, reading, or possessing of that book.

Contemplative and bookish men must of necessity be more quarrelsome than others, because neither do they contend about matters of fact nor can they determine their controversies by any certain witnesses or judges. But as long as they move towards peace (that is, truth), which way they take does not matter. The tutelary angels resisted one another in Persia, but none resisted God's revealed purpose (Dan. 10). Jerome and Gregory seem to be of the opinion that Solomon is damned; Ambrose and Augustine, that he is saved—all Fathers, all zealous of God's glory. At the same time when the Roman Church canonized Becket, the school of Paris disputed whether he could be saved; both Catholic judges, and of reverend authority. After so many ages of devoutly and religiously celebrating the memory of Saint Jerome, Casaubon has spoken so dangerously that Campion says he pronounces him to be as deep in hell as the devil. But in all such intricacies, where both opinions seem to conduce equally to the honor of God, his justice being as much advanced in the one as is his mercy in the other, it seems reasonable to me that it tips the scales, if on either side there appears charity toward the poor soul departed. The church in her hymns and antiphons often salutes Christ's nails and cross with epithets of sweetness and thanks, but it always calls the spear that pierced him when he was dead the horrible sword.

Such piety, I affirm again, urges me in this discourse. Whatever infirmity my reasons may have, still I have comfort in Tresmegistus's axiom, "He who is pious is the best philosophizer." Therefore, without any disguising or careful and libelous concealing, I present and expose it to all who have candor and neutrality, in order to escape the just reproof of Jerome, "A new kind of malice and intemperance is to communicate what you wish to hide." When Ladislas took the occasion of the Great Schism to corrupt the nobility of Rome and hoped thereby to possess the town, they added to their seven governors, whom they called wise men, three more, whom they called good men, and confided in them; so do I wish and, as much as I can, bring it about that to those many learned and subtle men who have traveled over this point, some charitable and compassionate men might be added.

Yosippon observes that readers are of four sorts: sponges that attract everything without distinguishing, hour-glasses that pour out as fast as they receive, bags that retain only the dregs of the spices and let the wine escape, and sieves that retain only the best. If I find some of the last sort, I do not doubt they may be enlightened. As the eyes of Eve were opened by the taste of the apple (although it is said she had already seen the beauty of the tree), so the digesting of this, though it may not present fair objects, may bring them to see the nakedness and deformity of their own reasons, founded upon a rigorous suspicion, and win them over to the temper that Chrysostom commends: "He who suspects benignly would fain be deceived and be overcome, and he is piously glad when he finds to be false what he uncharitably suspected." May it have as much vigor (as one observes of another author) as the sun in March; may it stir and dissolve humors—though not expel them, for that must be a work of a stronger power.

Not every branch that is excerpted from other authors and engrafted here is written for the reader to believe, but for the sake of illustration and comparison. Because I undertook the declaration of a proposition that was controverted by many—and therefore I was drawn to cite many authorities—I was willing to go all the way with company and to take light from others, as well in the journey as at the journey's end. If in multiplicity of unnecessary citations there appears vanity, or ostentation, or digression, my honesty must make my excuse and compensation. I acknowledge, as

Pliny does, "That to choose to be taken in a theft rather than to give every man his due" is to be low of mind and miserable of nature. I did it rather because scholastic and skillful men use this way of instructing, and I took into account that I was to deal with such, because I presume that natural men are of themselves at least enough inclinable to this doctrine.

This is my way, and my end is to remove scandal. Certainly God often punishes a sinner more severely because others have taken occasion of sinning from his deed. By the same token, if we corrected in ourselves this readiness to be scandalized, how much easier and lighter might we make the punishment of many transgressors? For God in his judgments has almost made us his assistants and counselors as to how far he will punish, and our interpretation of another's sin often gives the measure to God's justice or mercy.

Since "disorderly long hair, which was pride and wantonness in Absalom and squalor and horridness in Nebuchadnezzar, was virtue and strength in Solomon and sanctification in Samuel," if these severe men will not allow to neutral things the best construction they are capable of nor pardon my inclination to do so, surely they will pardon this opinion, that their severity proceeds from self-guiltiness, and will give me leave to apply the saying of Ennodius, "It is the nature of stiff wickedness to think of others what they themselves deserve, and all the comfort that the guilty have is to find nobody innocent."

THE FIRST PART: OF LAW AND NATURE

Distinction I

1. As lawyers used to call impossible what is so difficult that by the rules of law it can be accomplished only by the indulgence of the prince and the exercise of his prerogative, so divines are accustomed to call sin what mostly is so and naturally occasions and accompanies sin. Of such condition is self-homicide. Everybody has so sucked, digested, and incorporated it as a sin into the body of his faith and religion that now they forbid any opposition. Thus all discourse on this point turns on the degrees of this sin and how far it exceeds all others. So nobody now brings the metal to the test or the touch, but only to the balance. Whatever to our appetite is good or bad was first to our understanding true or false; therefore, if we might proceed orderly, our first disquisition should be employed upon the first source and origin—which is, whether this opinion is true or false. But, finding ourselves under the inequity and burden of this custom and prescription, we must yield to necessity and first inversely examine why this act should be so resolutely condemned and why there should be this precipitousness in our judgment to pronounce self-homicide to be above all other sins unpardonable. Then, having removed what was nearest to us and having delivered ourselves from the tyranny of this prejudice, our judgment may be brought nearer to a straightness and our charity awakened and made tender to apprehend that this act may be free not only from those enormous degrees but from *all* degrees of sin.

2. Those who pronounce this sin to be necessarily damnable are of one of these three persuasions. Either they misstate that this act always proceeds from desperation [i.e., despair of God's mercy], and so they load it with all the abundant denunciations available from scripture, Fathers, and histories. Or they entertain the dangerous opinion that there is in this life an inability to repent and an impossibility of returning to God, and that this is apparent to us; otherwise, the act could not justify our uncharitable censure. Or else they build upon the foundation that this act, being presumed to be sin, and all sin presumed to be unpardonable without repentance, this is therefore unpardonable because the sin itself precludes all ordinary ways of repenting it.

3. To those of the first group, if I might be as vainly subtle as they are uncharitably severe, I answer that not all desperation is sinful. For in

the devil it is not sin, nor does he suffer demerit from it, because he is
not commanded to hope. In a man who undertook an austere and disci-
plinary taming of his body by fasts or corrections it would not be sinful
to despair that God would take from him the desire of the flesh. In a
priest employed to convert infidels it would not be sinful to despair that
God would give him the power of miracles. If, therefore, to quench and
extinguish this desire of the flesh a man should kill himself, the effect
and fruit of this desperation would be evil; yet the root itself is not necessarily so. No detesting or exhorting against this sin of desperation,
when it *is* a sin, can be too earnest. But since it may exist without infidelity, it cannot be a greater sin than that is.

Although Aquinas calls it truly sin, he says he does so because it
occasions many sins. If, as others affirm, it is punishment for sin, then it
is involuntary, which is hardly consistent with the nature of sin. Certainly, many devout men have justly imputed to it the cause and effect
of sin; yet, as in the Penitential Canons greater penance is inflicted upon
one who kills his wife than upon one who kills his mother, and the reason added is not that the fault is greater but that otherwise more would
commit it, so is the sin of desperation so earnestly exaggerated because,
as it springs from sloth and cowardliness, our nature is more slippery and
inclinable to such a descent than to presumptions, which without a doubt
does more to wound and violate the majesty of God than desperation
does. However, so that none may justly say that all who kill themselves
have done it out of a despair of God's mercy (which is the only sinful
despair), we shall in a more proper place, when we come to consider the
examples exhibited in scriptures and other stories, find many who in that
act have been so far from despair that they have esteemed it a great
degree of God's mercy to have been admitted to such a glorifying of his
name and have proceeded therein as religiously as in a sacrifice. As
Bosquier says elegantly of Job, "He appears in splendid proverbs," and of
him we may properly say what Moses said when they punished one
another for their idolatries, "Consecrate your hands to the Lord" (Exod.
32:29).

I come to consider their words who are of the second opinion and who
affirm an inability to repent in this life. (A strong authorizer if not an
author of this opinion is Calvin, who says that actual unrepentance is not
the sin intimated in Matthew 12:30–31; rather, we must hold that whoever
falls into such a willful resistance of the Holy Ghost never rises again.)
Because these hard and misinterpretable words fall from them when they
are perplexed and enmeshed with that heavy question of sin against the
Holy Ghost, and because I presume to speak proportionally and analogi-
cally to their other doctrine, I rather incline to make for them this
construction: that they place this inability to repent only in the knowledge
of God—or that I do not understand them rather than either believe them

literally or believe that they have clearly expressed their own meanings. For I do not see why we should be more loath to allow that God has made some persons unable to sin than that he has made them unable to repent. Even if they had their way and this were granted to them, I cannot see that therefore such an inability to repent must necessarily be concluded to have been in a person by reason of self-homicide. and it gives great-

4. The third sort is the tamest of all the three, and it gives the greatest hope of being overcome and corrected. Although they pronounce severely upon the act, it is for the single reason that the act precludes all entrance into repentance. I wonder why they refuse to apply to their opinions in this matter the milder rules of the casuists, who in doubtful cases always teach an inclination to the safer side. While it is safer to think a thing to be sin than not, that rule serves for your own information and as a as a bridle to you, not for another's condemnation. They used to interpret that rule of taking the safer side so that in things necessary (necessary to an end, as repentance is necessary to salvation) we must follow any probable opinion, even if another is more probable, and so that opinion is to be followed directly which is favorable to the soul. They exemplify this point as follows. Although all the leading scholastics hold that baptizing a child, not yet fully born, on the hand or foot is ineffectual, still they all advise in that case to baptize and to believe it to be of good effect. The example of the good thief on the cross (Luke 23:43) informs us that repentance works immediately, and from that story Calvin gathers that such pain at the moment of death is naturally apt to beget repentance.

The church is so indulgent and liberal to all her children that at the point of death she will bestow her treasure of baptism upon one who has been insane from his birth, by the same reason as upon a child—indeed, upon one recently fallen into insanity, although he appears to be in mortal sin, if only he has attrition, which is only a fear of hell and not a taste of God's glory. Such attrition shall be presumed to be in him, if nothing appears evidently to the contrary. If the church is content to extend and interpret this point of death to every danger by sea or travel; if she will interpret any mortal sin in a man provoked by sudden passion and proceeding from indeliberation to be no worse and of no greater malignity than the act of a child; if, being able to succor one before he is dead, she will deliver him from excommunication after he is dead; if she is content that both the penitent and confessor are only diligent, not most diligent; if, rather than be frustrated in her desire to dispense her treasure, she grants that insane and possessed men shall be bound until they may receive extreme unction; if, lastly, she absolves some whether they wish it or not—in light of all this, why should we abhor our mother's example and as brethren be more severe than the parent? Not to pray for those who die without faith is a precept so obvious to every religion that even

Muhammad has forbidden it. But to presume an inability to repent
because you were not nearby to hear it is a usurpation.

True repentance, says Clement of Alexandria, is "To do no more and
to speak no more those things whereof you repent; it is not to be always
sinning and always asking pardon." Of such a repentance as this our case
is capable enough. Of one who died before he had repented the good
Paulinus charitably interprets his haste, "That he chose rather to go to
God a debtor than as free," and so to die in his debt rather than to carry
his discharge from it. Since in matters of fact the delinquent is so much
favored that a layman who acquits him is sooner to be believed than a
clergyman who accuses him—although in other cases there is much
disproportion between the value of these two testimonies—so, if any will
of necessity proceed to judgment in our case, those reasons that are most
benign and (as I said) favorable to the soul ought to have the best
acceptance and entertainment.

5. Of all those definitions of sin that the first collector of sentences,
Peter the Lombard, has presented out of ancient learning, the authors of
summas as well as the casuists insist most on the one that he gets from
Saint Augustine. As usual, where that Father serves their purposes they
look no further. This definition is that sin is a word, deed, or desire
against the eternal law of God. They stick to this definition (if it is one)
because it best supports their argument, because it is the easiest convey-
ance, carriage, and vent for their conceptions and for their applying
rules of divinity to particular cases. Thus they have made all our actions
perplexed and litigious in the inner court of conscience, which is their
tribunal. By this torture they have brought men's consciences to the
same reasons of complaint that Pliny attributes to Rome until Trajan's
time, that the city founded on the laws was being overturned by the
laws. For as informers vexed them with continual denunciations upon
penal laws, so does this act of sinning entangle wretched consciences in
manifold and desperate anxieties.

This use of the definition cannot be thought to apply only to sin,
since it limits sin to the eternal law of God. (This term, although not in
Peter the Lombard, Sayer and all the rest retain.) This eternal law of
God is the ground of the governance of God, no other than his eternal
decree for the government of the whole world; that is, providence. Certainly a man may without sin both speak and act against providence,
since it is not always revealed, just as I may resist a disease from which
God has decreed that I shall die. Even though he seems to reveal his will,
we may resist it with prayers against it, because it is often conditioned
and accompanied by limitations and exceptions. Even though God dealt
plainly with Nathan, saying, "The child shall surely die" (I Sam. 12:14),
David resisted God's decree by prayer and penance.

We must therefore seek another definition of sin. I think it is not as well put in those words of Aquinas, "Every failure to perform an obligation has the character of sin," as in his other definition, "Sin is an act departing from the ordained end, against the rule of nature or of reason, or of eternal law." Here eternal law, being stated as a member and part of the definition, cannot admit of the vast and large interpretation that it could not escape in the description of Saint Augustine; in this text it must necessarily be intended as the divine law of scripture. Through this definition, therefore, we will grace this act of self-homicide and see whether it offends any of those three sorts of law.

6. Of all these three laws—of nature, of reason, and of God—every precept that is permanent and always binds is so composed, elemented, and complexioned that to distinguish and separate them is an alchemistic work. Either it only seems to be done or it is done by the torture and vexation of scholastic nit-pickings [original: "school-limbicks," a racking of the brain over abstract ideas], which are abstruse and violent distinctions. The part of God's law that always binds already bound before it was written, and so it is simply the rule of rectified reason, and that is the law of nature. Therefore Isidore of Seville (as it is related in the canons), dividing all law into divine and human, adds, "Divine consists of nature, human of custom."

Although these three laws are almost entirely one, yet because one thing may be commanded in various ways and by various authorities—as the common law, a statute, and a decree of an arbitrary court may bind me to do the same thing—it is necessary that we weigh the obligation of every one of these laws that is in the definition.

But first I shall only soften and prepare their crude, undigested opinions and prejudice, which may be contracted from the frequent iteration and specious but sophisticated inculcatings of law—of nature, reason, and God—by this antidote: many things that are of natural, human, and divine law may be broken. To conceal a secret delivered to you is of this sort. The honor due to parents is so strictly one of these laws that none of the Second Table (Exod. 20:12–17) is more so, yet in a just war a parricide is not guilty. Indeed, according to a law of Venice—though Bodin says better the town were sunk than that this ever should be an example or precedent—a son must redeem himself from banishment by killing his father who is also banished. We read of another state (and laws of civil commonwealths may not lightly be pronounced to be against nature) where, when fathers came to be of an unprofitable and useless age, the sons must beat them to death with clubs. We read of still another where all persons above seventy years were dispatched.

7. This term, the law of nature, is so variously and inconsistently defined that I confess I must read it a hundred times before I understand it once or can conclude that it signifies what the author at that time means. Yet I never found it in any sense that might justify their vociferations upon

sins against nature. For the transgressing of the law of nature in any act
seems to me not to increase the heinousness of that act, as though nature
were more obligatory than divine law. Only in one respect does natural law
aggravate a transgression; that is, in such a sin we are inexcusable by any
pretense of ignorance, since we can discern it by the light of nature. Many
things that we call sin (and therefore evil) have been done by the
commandment of God; for example, by Abraham (Gen. 22:2) and by the
Israelites in their departing from Egypt (Exod. 12:35). Thus the evil is
neither in the nature of the thing nor in the nature of the whole harmony of
the world. Therefore, evil inheres in no law of nature but in violating or
omitting a commandment.

All is obedience or disobedience. Wherefore our countryman Sayer
confesses that self-homicide is not as intrinsically evil as it is to lie. This
point is also evident from Cajetan, who affirms that to save my life I
may not accuse myself from the rack. Although Cajetan extends the
matter no further than that I may not belie myself, Soto refuses
Cajetan's reasons with so much force as to forbid any self-accusation,
even though it is true. Thus, according to Cajetan, I may depart from
life much more easily than from truth or fame. But we find that many
holy men have been very negligent of their fame. Not only Augustine,
Anselm, and Jerome betrayed themselves by unurged confessions; Saint
Ambrose even procured certain prostitute women to come into his
chamber so that he might be defamed and the people would thereby
abstain from making him their bishop.

Intrinsic and natural evil can hardly be found! For God, who can
command a murder, cannot command an evil or a sin. Since the whole
frame and government of the world is his, he may use it as he will. For
example, although he can do a miracle, he can do nothing against
nature, because "That is the nature of everything which he works in it,"
says Augustine. From this and from that other rule of Aquinas's, "Whatever is wrought by a superior agent upon a patient who is naturally
subject to that agent is natural," we may safely infer that nothing we
call sin is so against nature that it may not sometimes be agreeable to
nature.

On the other side, nature is often taken so widely and so extensively
that all sin is very truly said to be against nature—even before it comes
to be sin. Saint Augustine says, "Every vice, so far as it is a vice, is
against nature." Vice is only habit that, being extended into act, is then
sin. Yes, the parent of all sin, which is hereditary, original sin, which
Aquinas calls "a languor and faintness in our nature and an indisposition,
proceeding from the dissolution of the harmony of original justice," is
said by him to be in us "as if natural" and is, as he says in another place,
so natural "that although it is propagated with our nature in generation,
it is not caused by the principles of nature." Thus, if God should now

miraculously frame a man, as he did the first woman, from another's flesh and bone (and not by generation) into that creature, all the infirmities of our flesh would be derived, but not original sin. Original sin is transmitted by nature only, and, since all actual sin issues from it, all sin is natural.

8. To approach nearer, let us leave the consideration of the law of nature in this sense of providence and God's decree for his government of the great world, and reduce it simply to the law of nature in the lesser world of ourselves. There is in us a double law of nature, sensitive and rational, and the first naturally leads and conduces to the other. Because by the languor and faintness of our nature we lazily rest there and for the most part go no further in our journeys, out of this ordinary disposition Aquinas pronounces that the inclination of our sensitive nature is against the law of reason. This is what the apostle calls the law of the flesh and what he opposes to the law of the spirit (Rom. 7:23).

Although it is possible to sin and to transgress against this sensitive nature, which naturally and lawfully is inclined toward a desirable good, by denying it lawful refreshings and promptings, still I think this is not the law of nature that those who abhor self-homicide complain is violated by that act. They might as well accuse all discipline, all austerity, and all love of martyrdom, which are just as contrary to the law of sensitive nature.

9. Therefore by the law of nature, if they will mean anything and speak to be understood, they must intend the law of rational nature, which is the light that God has given of his eternal law. It is usually called rectified reason. Now since this law of nature exists only in man and directs him toward piety, religion, and sociableness—so far as it reaches to the preservation of the species and of individuals, there are lively prints of it in beasts—most authors confound it and make it the same with the law of nations. So says Azorius. Sylvius writes that "the law of nature as it concerns only reason is the law of nations." Therefore, whatever is the law of nations, that is, practiced and accepted, most especially in civilized nations, is also the law of nature, which Artemidorus exemplifies in these two, to serve God and to be overcome by women.

How then shall we accuse idolatry or immolation of being sins against nature? (I will not speak of the first, which like a deluge overflowed the world, and only Canaan was a little ark swimming in it, delivered from utter drowning—but not from storms, leaks, and dangerous weather-beatings.) Immolation of men was so ordinary that "almost every nation, although not barbarous, had received it." The Druids of France made their divinations from sacrifices of men, and in their wars they foretold the future in the same way. In our times it appears, according to the Spanish reports, that in Hispaniola alone they sacrificed yearly 20,000 children.

10. However, since it is received from Aquinas that "The nature of

every thing is the form by which it is continued, and to act against it is to act against nature," and since also this form in man is reason, and to act against reason is to sin against nature, what sin can be exempt from the charge that it is a sin against nature, since every sin is against reason? In this sense Lucidus takes the law of nature when he says, "God has written in our hearts such a law of nature as by that we are saved in the coming of Christ." Thus, every act that does not agree exactly with our religion will be a sin against nature. This will appear evidently from Jeremiah's words, where God promises as a future blessing that he will write his laws in their hearts, which is the Christian law (Jer. 31:33).

The Christian law and the law of nature (for that is the law written in hearts) must be the same. Sin therefore against nature is not so enormous but that what Navarrus says may stand true, "Many laws both natural and divine bind only to what is pardonable." (I am not disputing at this time whether or not it is always against reason, for reason and virtue differ exactly as do a closed box of drugs and a plaster or medicine made from them and applied to a particular use and necessity; in the box are not only aromatic medicinals but also many poisons made wholesome by the nature of the disease and the art of the one who administers them.) By the same token, self-homicide is no more against the law of nature than any other sin, not in any of the interpretations that we touched upon above.

This is as much as I determined for this first distinction.

Distinction II

1. There is a lower and narrower interpretation of this law of nature (which could not well be discerned except in light of the foregoing discussion), against which law this sin and very few others seem to be directly bent and opposed. Azorius says, "There are sins peculiarly against nature that are against the natural practice of men," which he exemplifies in unnatural lusts and in self-homicide. Of the former example Aquinas says, "There are some kinds of lusts that are sins against nature both as they are generally vices and as they are against the natural order of the act of generation." In the scriptures the sin of misusing sex is called against nature by Saint Paul (Rom. 1:26–27) and once in the Vulgate edition in the Old Testament (Judges 19:24). But, as I intimated once before, this sin against nature is so much abhorred not because its being against nature makes it so abominable but because the knowledge thereof is so domestic, so near, so inward to us that our conscience cannot slumber in it nor dissemble it, as it does in most sins.

Take the example of the Levite in the book of Judges (19:1ff.). Let's assume that those wicked men did seek him for that abominable use—although Josephus says it was only for his wife, and when he himself relates to the people the story of his injury in the next chapter, he complains only that they went about to kill him to enjoy his wife and of no other kind of injury. Although the host who had harbored him tried to dissuade the men, saying, "Only let nothing be done that is against nature," will any man say that the offer he made to extinguish their furious lust, to expose them to his own daughter, a virgin, and the wife of his guest (which Josephus increases by calling her a Levite and his kinswoman) was a lesser sin than to have given way to their violence, or less against nature, because what they sought was against natural practice?

Is not every voluntary pollution in the genus of sin as much against the law of nature as this was, since it strays and departs from the way and defeats the end of that faculty in us, which is generation? In no interpretation does the violating of the law of nature aggravate the sin. Neither does the scripture call any sin other than disorderly lust by that name. Saint Paul once appeals to the law of nature, when arguing about the covering of the heads of men or women at public prayer. He says, "Judge for yourselves," and, "Does not nature teach you that if a man has long hair it is a shame?" (I Cor. 11:13–14). Not that this was against that law of nature to which all men are bound, for it was not always so. In most places shavings, cuttings, and pullings of hair are reprehended for delicacy and effeminacy by the satirists and epigrammatists of those times. Until foreign corruption poisoned them, the Romans were always gloriously called unshorn. But, says Calvin, "Because it was at that time received as a custom throughout all Greece to wear short hair, Saint Paul calls it natural."

So Vegetius says, "From November to March the seas are shut up and unmanageable by the law of nature, which now are tame and manageable enough, and this is also by the law of nature." And the custom that Saint Paul called natural in Greece was not long natural there. For the bishops of Rome, when they made their canons regulating priest's shavings, did it because they wanted their priests to differ from the priests of the Greek Church. So Saint Paul's mentioning the law of nature does not argue from the weight and heinousness of the fault, as our adversaries use it, but he uses it as the nearest, most familiar, and easiest way to lead them to a knowledge of decency and to a departing from scandalous singularity in those public meetings.

2. Although Azorius (as I said) and many others make self-homicide an example of sin in particular against the law of nature, it is only for the reason that self-preservation is of natural law. But that natural law is so general that it applies to beasts more than to us, because they cannot compare degrees of obligation and distinctions of duties and offices, as we can. We know from Aquinas that "some things are natural to the species and other things to the particular person" and that the latter may correct the former. Thus, when Cicero consulted the oracle at Delphi, he

had this answer, "Follow your own nature." Certainly the text, "It is not good for the man to be alone" (Gen. 2:18) is meant there, because if he were alone God's purpose of multiplying mankind would have been frustrated. Though it would be bad for the conservation of our species in general, it may be very fitting for some particular man to abstain from all such consorting in marriage or with men and to retire into solitude. Some may need Chrysostom's counsel, "Depart from the highway and transplant yourself in some enclosed ground, for it is hard for a tree that stands by the wayside to keep its fruit till it is ripe."

Our safest assurance that we will not be misled by the ambiguity of the term, natural law, and by the perplexed variety of its use in authors will be this from Aquinas: "All the precepts of natural law result in these: flee evil; seek good." That is to say, act according to reason.

As these precepts are not dispensable by any authority, so they cannot be abolished or obscured, for our hearts will always not only retain but also acknowledge this law. From these precepts are deduced by consequence others that are not always necessary, such as, "Return a deposit." Although this seems to follow from the first rule (act according to reason), it is not always just. Aquinas says that the lower you go towards particulars the more you depart from the necessity of being bound to it. Ennenckel illustrates it more clearly, "It is natural and binds all always to know that there is a God. From this it is deduced by necessary consequence that God (if he is) must be worshiped and then by likely consequence that he must be worshiped in this or that manner." So, a little corruptly and adulterately, every sect will call their discipline natural law and enjoin a necessary obedience to it.

While our *substance* of nature (the foundations and principles and first grounds of natural law) may not be changed, yet the *function* of nature (the exercise and application of those principles) and deductions therefrom may and must be changed. A similar danger lies in deducing consequences from the natural law of self-preservation, which does not bind so rigorously, urgently and unlimitedly as to preclude that by the law of nature itself living things may, indeed must, neglect themselves for others. Of this the pelican [believed to have fed its young its own blood] is an instance or emblem. Saint Ambrose, philosophizing divinely in a contemplation of bees, after he has afforded them many other praises, says, "When they find themselves guilty of having broken any of their king's laws, they injure themselves, condemned to punishment, that they may die from their own wound." This magnanimity and justice he compares with that of the subjects of the kings of Persia, who in similar cases are their own executioners. Like this natural instinct in beasts, so rectified reason, belonging only in us, instructs us often to prefer public and necessary persons by exposing ourselves to inevitable destruction.

No law is so primary and simple that it does not preconceive a reason upon which it was founded, and hardly any reason is too constant for circumstances to alter it. In that case, a private man is emperor over himself; so a devout man, Dorotheus, interprets those words, "Let us create man in our own image, that is, to be judge in his own cause." He whose conscience, well-tempered and dispassionate, assures him that the reason of self-preservation ceases for him may also presume that the law ceases too, and may do what otherwise would be against that law.

If it is true that "It belongs to the bishop of Rome to declare, interpret, limit, and distinguish the law of God," as their authorities teach, which is to declare when the reason of the law ceases, what this author and the canons affirm may be just as true, that he may dispense with that law; he does no more than any man might do with respect to himself, if he could judge as infallibly. Let it be true that no man may at any time do anything against the law of nature; still, Aquinas says, "Dispensation does not work so that I may use it to disobey a law, but so that this law becomes to me no law in the case where the reason of it ceases." So may any man be bishop and magistrate over himself and dispense with his conscience, where it can appear that the reason—that is, the soul and form—of the law has ceased.

As in oaths and vows, so in the law, the necessity of dispensations proceeds from the fact that a thing which, when universally considered in itself, is profitable and honest, by reason of some particular event becomes either dishonest or hurtful. Neither of these events can fall within the reach or under the commandment of any law. In these exempt and privileged cases, "The privilege is not against universal law but against the universality of law," according to Ennenckel. It only relieves a person, it does not wound or render infirm a law, any more than I diminish the virtue of light or the dignity of the sun if, to escape its scorching, I allow myself the relief of the shade.

Neither the watchfulness of parliaments nor the descents and indulgences of princes who have consented to laws derogatory to themselves has been able to prejudice the prince's "notwithstandings," because prerogative is incomprehensible. It overflows and transcends all law. Just as those canons that boldly and, according to some schoolmen, blasphemously say, "The pope is not allowed," neither diminish the fulness of his power nor impeach the motions proper to him (as they call them) or his "notwithstanding divine law," because they are understood always to whisper some just reservation—without just cause, or in matters as they stand—so, whatever law is cast upon the conscience or liberty of man, of which the reason is mutable, is naturally conditioned in that it binds only so long as the reason lives.

Moreover, self-preservation, which we confess to be the foundation of general natural law, is nothing other than a natural affection and desire for good, whether real or apparent. Certainly the motive for martyrdom, although the body perishes, is self-preservation, because thereby out of our election to salvation our best part is advanced. Heaven, which we thus gain, is certainly good, while this life is only probably and possibly good. What Athenagoras says holds well here, "Earthly things and heavenly things so differ as verisimilitude and truth." And Pico's is the best description of felicity that I have found, "It is the return of any given thing to its origin."

Now this law of self-preservation is accomplished in attaining what conduces to our ends and is good to us, for liberty, which is a faculty of doing what I would, is as much of the law of nature as preservation is. Still, if for reasons seeming good to me, such as to preserve my life when I am justly taken prisoner if I will become a slave, I may do it without violating the law of nature. If I propose to myself in self-homicide a greater good, even though I mistake it, I do not see how I transgress the general law of nature, which is an affection for good, whether real or apparent. If what I effect by death is truly a greater good, how is the other, stricter law of nature, which is rectified reason, violated?

3. Another reason that prevails much with me and keeps self-homicide from being against the law of nature is this: in all ages, in all places, and upon all occasions men of all conditions have wanted it and inclined to do it. As Cardan says, "Metal is a buried plant, and a mole is a buried animal." So man, as though he were a buried angel, labors to be discharged of his earthly sepulchre, his body. To be sure, it may be said of all other sins that men are prone to them, and despite their frequency they are against nature—that is, rectified reason. Still, if this sin were in particular against the law of nature (as they must hold who make it worse by that circumstance) such that it worked to the destruction of our species in any other way than do intemperate lust, gluttony, or incurring penal laws, and the like, it could not be as general as they are. For, being contrary to our sensitive nature, it lacks the advantage of pleasure or delight to allure us that other sins have.

When I frame for myself a martyrology of all who have perished by their own means for the sake of religion, country, fame, love, ease, fear, and shame, I blush to see how naked all the other virtues are in comparison with fortitude; I blush to see that all the stories do not afford so many examples (either of cunning and subtle stratagems or of forcible and violent actions) for safeguarding life as they do for destroying it.

Petronius Arbiter, who served Nero, a man of pleasure, in the office of master of his pleasures, at the first frown of displeasure went home and cut his veins. To him so present and immediate a step was it from full pleasure to such a death.

How subtly and curiously Atilius Regulus destroyed himself! Being of such integrity that he would never have lied to save his life, he lied to lose it, falsely pleading that the Carthaginians had given him poison, and that within a few days he should die—although he stayed at Rome.

Codrus's forcing of his own death exceeded even this, because in the disguise of a common soldier he was likely to perish without fame.

Herennius the Sicilian could endure beating out his own brains against a post. As though he owed thanks to the brain that had given him this device of killing himself, he would not leave off beating until he could see it and salute it.

Comas, who had been a captain of thieves, came to the torture of trial. Scorning all foreign and accessory aids to dying, he made his own breath the instrument of his death by holding it.

Hannibal, who would be beholden to none for life or death, lest he should be overtaken by extreme necessity died from poison that he always carried in a ring.

So did Demosthenes die from poison he carried in a pen.

When Aristarchus saw that neither his seventy-two years of age nor the corrupt and malignant disease of being a severe critic could wear him out, he starved himself to death.

Homer, who had written a thousand things that nobody else understood, is said to have hanged himself because he did not understand the fisherman's riddle.

Othryades, of the 300 champions appointed to end a quarrel between the Lacedemonians and the Athenians, alone survived; when the lives of all the 300 were then in him, as though it would be a new victory to kill them once again, he killed himself.

Damocles, whom a Greek tyrant would have violated, in order to show that he could suffer any other heat scalded himself to death.

Cato's daughter Porcia, like Catulus, opposed new measures—Quintilian calls them "new causes for dying"—and died by swallowing burning coals.

Poor Terence, because he lost his 108 translated comedies, drowned himself.

And the poet Labienus, because his satirical books were burned by edict, burnt himself too.

Zeno, over whom hardly any is preferred, stumbled and hurt his finger against the ground. He interpreted that as a summons from the earth and hanged himself, being then almost 100 years old. For this act Diogenes Laertius proclaims him to have been "A man who departed this life in great happiness, sound, whole, and without illness."

To cure himself of fever, Porcius Latro killed himself.

Festus, Domitian's minion, did it only to hide the deformity of a ringworm in his face.

Hipponax the poet rhymed Bupalus the painter to death with his iambics.

Licinius Macer bore well enough being called into question for great faults, but he hanged himself when he heard that Cicero would plead against him, although the Roman condemnations at that time did not inflict such heavy punishments.

Cassius Licinius, to escape Cicero's judgment, by choking himself with a napkin had, as Tacitus calls it, "the reward of hastening his death."

You can hardly imagine any person so happy or miserable, so reposed or so vain, or any occasion either of true loss or shame or perversity, for which there are no examples of it. Yet nobody seems to me to have made harder shift to die than Charondas, who made a new law punishing by death whoever entered the council chamber armed; then he broke that law and soon punished himself by falling upon his sword.

The general desire for such death is abundantly expressed in those swarms of Roman gladiatory champions who, Lucidus reckons, in one month cost Europe 30,000 men. Not only men of great birth and place in the state but also women coveted to be admitted to its exercise and outpouring of life, until express laws forbade it.

From Eleazar's oration, recorded in Josephus, we may see how small persuasions moved men to this act; "He only told them that the philosophers among the Indians did so, and that we and our children were born to die but not born to be slaves."

We may well recall that, in Caesar's time in France, for every one who died naturally there died many by this devout violence. He says there were some, whom he calls devotees and clients (the later laws call them vassals) who, enjoying many benefits and commodities from men of higher rank, when the lord died always celebrated his funeral with their own. Caesar adds that in the memory of man no one was found who ever refused it.

This devotion, I have read somewhere, continues still in all the wives in the kingdom of Bengal in India. There not only such persons do it in testimony of an entire dependency and gratitude, but also the Samanaians, who did not inherit religious rank, priesthood, and wisdom as did the Levites among the Jews and the Gymnosophists among them, but these were admitted to it by election, when notice was taken of their sanctity. They are said to have studied ways how to die, especially when they were in the best state of health. These priests, whose care was to die thus, always summed up and abridged all their precepts into this one, "Let a pious death determine a good life." In such estimation they held this manner of dying.

How pathetically Latinus Pacatus expresses the sweetness of dying when we will! "Others," says he, "after the conquest, making a braver bargain with destiny, prevented uncertain death by certain death, and the slaves escaped whipping by strangling themselves. For whoever feared that after death there was no hope? Or who would therefore forbear to kill himself whom another might kill? Is another's hand easier than your own? Or is a private death fouler than a public one? Or is it more pain to fall on your sword and to press the wound with your body—and so receive death at once—than to divide the torment, bend the knee, stretch out the neck, perhaps to more than one blow?" Then, wondering why Maximus, who had murdered the emperor Gratian and was now subdued by Theodosius, had not enjoyed the common benefit of killing himself, he (Pacatus) turns upon Gratian and says, "Reverend Gratian, you have chased your executioner and would not allow him leisure for so honest a death, lest he should stain the sacred, imperial robe with such impious blood, or a tyrant's hand should perform your revenge, or you be beholden to him for his own death." With similar passion speaks another panegyric to Constantine, who after a victory took from the conquered their swords, lest anyone come to grief. From this language one may see how natural it was in those times to prefer such dispatch.

In our age, when the Spaniards extended the law that was made only against the cannibals, so that those who would not accept the Christian religion should incur bondage, the Indians in infinite numbers escaped this slavery by killing themselves. They never ceased until the Spaniards by some deceptions made them think they also would kill themselves and follow the Indians with some severity into the next life.

This much seems to me sufficient to defeat the argument that is drawn from self-preservation and to prove that it is not so much in particular a law of nature that it is not often transgressed naturally.

Here we will end this second distinction.

Distinction III

1. After this, when men by civility and mutual use of one another became more thrifty of themselves and sparing of their lives, the solemnity of killing themselves at funerals wore out and vanished, but slowly and by insensible diminutions. "For first as a symbol of it the men wounded themselves and the women scratched and defaced their cheeks and sacrificed by that sprinkling of blood. After that, they made graves for themselves near their friends' graves and entered into them alive as nuns do when they renounce the world. Then as a symbol of this symbol they only took some earth and wore it upon their heads, and so for the public benefit they were content to forfeit their custom of dying," according to Sylvius.

Then came Christianity. Besides its many advantages over other philosophies, it has made us clearly understand the state of the next life. (Although Moses and his followers understood it, they always disguised it under earthly rewards and punishments, either because human nature from its first fall to its restitution and dignification by Christ was generally incapable of understanding such mysteries, or because it was reserved to our blessed savior to interpret and comment upon his own law, which that great successive trinity of human wisdom, Socrates, Plato, and Aristotle, saw only glimmeringly and variously. As to matters of this life, Christianity is the most Stoic and severe sect that ever cast bridle upon mankind.) I say, after Christianity had quenched those regards for fame, ease, shame, and such, how quickly and naturally man snatched and embraced a new way of expending his life by martyrdom!

2. There were the famous acts or famous sufferings of the Jews, even to defend their ceremonies. Many thousands of them were slain simply because they would not defend themselves on the sabbath (I Macc. 2:31–38). The customs of that nation were always steeped in sacrifices of blood. Of almost all other nations they were the most devout and earnest, even in the immolation of men. There is the example of our blessed savior, who chose as the way for our redemption to sacrifice his life and shed his blood. While all this was fresh in the minds of the early Christians and governed all their affections, it was not hard for their authorities, even by natural reasons and examples, to invite or to cherish their propensity to martyrdom.

Therefore, when Clement of Alexandria handles this matter, he presents hardly any argument other than natural men are capable of, and such food and fuel as would serve the taste and fervor of one who was not curious beyond nature. For example, he argues thus: that death was not naturally evil; that the heathen endured greater pains for less reward; that a barbarous people immolated every year a principal philosopher to Zamolxis an idol, and those upon whom the lot fell did not mourn that fact; with most earnestness, that martyrdom is within our own power—all of which are arguments better proportioned to nature than to divinity. Clement presumed that the early Christians were persons inclined or inclinable by nature to this affection.

Tertullian's reasons are somewhat more sublime, yet rather fine and delightful than solid and weighty. For example, he argues thus: that God, knowing that man would sin after baptism, provided him a second solace, the baptism of blood; that the death of the saints, which is said to be precious in God's sight, cannot be understood of the natural death common to all; that, from the beginning in Abel, righteousness was afflicted. These reasons would not have entered the heads of any in whom a natural inclination had not already opened the gates.

Cyprian takes the same path and insists upon applying prophecies of two sorts, that the early Christians should be despised in this world, and that they should be rewarded in the next.

To these were added external honors, annually celebrating their memories and entitling their deaths birthdays, and the early instituting of the office of notaries to regulate their passions—even in Clement of Rome's time; also, the proposing that their embalmed heads be worshiped, which term (although Eunapius spoke it profanely) was not undeserved by the general misuse of such devotion.

After the monopoly of appropriating martyrdom and bestowing its benefits only upon those who held the integrity of the faith and were in unity with the church, of which persuasion Augustine and Jerome and most of the ancients are said to be, came a continual increase in the dignity and merit of it, such as that by virtue of the performance of the act it purged actual sin, as baptism did original sin, even for one without charity and in schism. If it did not merit salvation, it diminished the intenseness of damnation. By these means they incited man's nature to it. The proneness might also have been a little corruptly warmed towards it by always seeing those punished who afflicted them, for Tertullian says, "No city escaped punishment that had shed Christian blood."

After this, they went on to admit more into the martyrs' fellowship and to confer and extend their privileges. By such indulgence are the innocents slain by Herod (Matt. 2:16) counted as martyrs. So is John the Baptist, although he did not die (Matt. 14:1-12, Mark 6:14-29) for a matter of Christian faith. So is he who suffers for any virtue. So is he who dies in his mother's womb if she is a martyr. So is he who, having been mortally wounded for his Christian profession, recovers. So is he who, being not mortally wounded, dies afterwards of sickness contracted by his own negligence, if that negligence did not amount to mortal sin.

So, not only the sickly and infirm later ages but even the purest times cherished in men this desire of death, even for contrary reasons; notwithstanding by change of circumstances, both reasons had the appearance of good. For as fire is made more intense sometimes by sprinkling water and sometimes by adding fuel, so when their teachers found any coolness or remissness in them and an inclination to flight or compromise with the state, then Cyprian noted such with the ignominy of *Libellatici*—buyers of forged certificates—because they had gotten false papers from the state. He says of them, "The fault of those Christians who made pagan sacrifices is less, not that their conscience is clean." Tertullian equally decries both fleeing and buying such papers when he says, "Persecution must not be redeemed, for running away is a buying of your peace for nothing, and a buying of your peace for money is a running away."

Then we shall find that, even against the plain meaning of the word martyr [i.e., a witness], it became the common opinion that death was requisite and necessary to make one a martyr. So in Eusebius the Christians, although afflicted, modestly refused the name of martyrs and professed that they did not deserve it, unless they were killed.

Contrariwise, in other times, the disease of headlong dying at once seemed both to wear down their numbers and to lay some scandal upon the cause that worked such a desire in men who did not understand why they did it; the uninstructed, the uncatechized, yes the unbaptized did only what they saw others do. The charity of the survivors imputed to them a baptism of water, as they hoped, or at least of blood, for that they saw! I say, as a learned writer of our time says, "The church abstains from easy canonizing, so that sanctity should not be devalued"— and sanctity here means sainthood, not holiness. Lest the dignity of martyrdom should be debased by such promiscuous admittance to it, they were often content to allow them the comfort of martyrdom without dying, which was only a returning to the natural sense of the word.

Ignatius in his letters calls himself a martyr. Yes, more than the rest he brought down the value of martyrdom and the costly price, for he says, "As he who honors a prophet in the name of a prophet shall have a prophet's reward (Matt. 10:41), so he shall have a martyr's honor who honors one who has been bound to Christ." As our most blessed savior was proceeding in his merciful purpose of increasing his kingdom on earth while permitting the heathen princes to continue theirs, the Christian religion was dilated and oppressed. Then its professors, so dejected and worn with confiscations and imprisonments, thought that, as in the passover from Egypt every door was sprinkled with blood (Exod. 12:7), so heaven had no door from this world except by fires, crosses, and bloody persecutions. Presuming heaven to be at the next step, they would often stubbornly or stupidly wink and so make that one step.

God forbid that any should be so malignant as to misinterpret me, as though I either thought the blood of martyrs was not the seed of the church or diminished their dignity. Yet it befits candor to confess that those times were afflicted with a disease of this natural desire for such a death, and that to such may fruitfully be applied those words of the good Paulinus, "The athlete does not win just because he undresses, nor do they swim to the far shore just because they strip off their clothes." Alas! We may sink and drown at the last stroke. To sail to heaven it is not enough to cast away the burdensome superfluities that we have long carried about us, but we must also take in a good freight. It is not lightness but an even-reposed steadfastness that carries us there.

Cyprian was forced to search out an answer to this lamentation, which he then found to be common to men on their death-beds, "We mourn because with all our strength we had vowed ourselves to martyrdom, of which we are deprived, being prevented by natural death." For those who offered themselves to martyrdom before they were called upon he is fain to provide the glorious and satisfying name of professors.

From such an inordinate desire, all too obedient to nature, proceeded the fury of some Christians who, standing by when sentence was pronounced against others, cried out, "We also are Christians." And that inexcusable zeal of Germanicus, who drew the beast to himself and forced it to tear his body! Why did he do this? Eusebius gives us his reason, that he might sooner be delivered out of this wicked and sinful life. These acts Eusebius glorifies with the praise that "They did them with a mind worthy of a philosopher." It seems that the wisest men provoked this act by their examples. At the burning of the temple at Jerusalem, Meirus son of Belgas and Josephus son of Delaeus, although they had access to the Romans, cast themselves into the fire.

How passionately Ignatius solicits the Roman Christians not to interrupt his death. "I fear," he says, "your charity will hurt me and make me begin my life all over again, unless you strive that it may be sacrificed now. I profess to all churches that I die willingly." After that, "Let me stroke the wild beasts with soothing words; let me entice and corrupt the beasts to devour me and to be my sepulcher; let me enjoy those beasts whom I wish were much more cruel than they are, and if they will not attack me, I will provoke and attract them by force." What was Ignatius's reason for this, being a man necessary to those churches and having allowable excuses for avoiding it? "Because to me it is more useful to die."

Such intemperance prompted the woman of Edessa, when the Emperor Valens had forbidden the Christians one temple to which particular reasons of devotion attracted them. When the officers asked her, "Why so squalid?" as she headlong dragged her son through the streets, to enrage them with this contumely she replied, "I do it lest, when you have slain all the other Christians, I and my son should come too late to partake of that benefit."

Such a disorderly heat possessed that old, wretched man who, passed by after the execution of a whole legion of 6,666 by iterated decimation [i.e., by repeatedly drawing lots and slaying every tenth soldier] under Maximinian. Although he was told that they died for resisting not only the Roman religion but also the state, for all that he wished that he might have the happiness to be with them, and so he extorted a martyrdom. For that age had grown so hungry and ravenous for it that many were baptized only because they would be burned, and children were taught to vex and provoke executioners so they might be thrown into the fire.

This assuredness that men, fully persuaded that they were doing well, would naturally run to this act made the proconsul in Africa exclaim, "Are there any more Christians who desire to die?" When a whole multitude by general voice disclosed themselves, he bade them, "Go hang and drown yourselves, and ease the magistrate." This natural disposition afforded Muhammad an argument against the Jews: "If your religion is so good, why do you not die for it?" Our primitive church was so enamored of death and so satisfied with it that, in order to vex and torture them more, the magistrate made laws to take from them the comfort of dying and increased their persecution by stopping it. They gloried in their numbers.

As in other warfares men muster and reckon how many they bring into the field, their confidence of victory was in the multitudes of those who were lost. In this interest they admitted into the catalogue of martyrs the infants slain by Herod and the 11,000 virgins. When 9,000 soldiers under Hadrian are said to have embraced the Christian religion by apparition of an angel, and when the emperor sent others to execute them, 1,000 of the executioners joined them, and so the whole 10,000 were crucified. Baronius speaks of the 10,000 executed in Armenia, celebrated on the twenty-second day of June—whether or not these are different from the 10,000 under Hadrian I have not investigated. Saint Gregory says, "Let God number our martyrs, for to us they are more in number than the sands." Baronius says that except for the first of January (for which the Roman martyrology records as many as most other days), there is no day that has less than 500 martyrs and almost every one has 900 or 800.

3. The church increased abundantly under all these pressures. For in profane and secular wars the greater the triumphs of a conqueror, the greater also are his armies, because then more and more concur to his splendor and participate in his fortunes. So in this spiritual warfare the greater the triumphant church was, the greater grew the militant church, each assisted by the prayers of the other. Although I still say that very many died out of a natural infirmity of despising this life, a great number had their direct sights on the glory of God and went to it fully awares. When all these treadings down only harrowed our savior's field and prepared and improved it for his harvest, the blood of the martyrs having (as Nicephorus Callistus says) almost strangled the devil, he tried to turn them away from this inclination by his two greatest instruments (when they are his), the magistrates and the learned.

By suggesting to the magistrate that their zeal to die grew only from their faith in the resurrection, the devil procured their bodies to be burnt and their ashes scattered into rivers, to frustrate and defeat that expectation. And he raised up subtle heretics to weaken and darken the virtue and majesty of martyrdom.

Of these the most pestilently cunning was Basileides. Suspecting in advance that he would not easily remove the desire of dying that nature had bred and custom confirmed in them, he tried to remove the desire that had root only in their religion, being of tenderer growth and more removable than natural impressions. He offered not to impugn their exposing themselves to death in all cases, but only said that it was madness to die for Christ, since he, by whose example they did it, was not crucified, but instead Simon who bore the cross. Another heretic called Elkesai, perceiving that it was too hasty to condemn the act of martyrdom even for Christ, thought only to slacken their desire for it by teaching that in time of persecution, as long as we kept our heart at anchor safe, we were not bound to testify to our religion by any outward act, much less by dying.

This doctrine the Gnostics also taught, because the contrary was rooted in nature, because they accompanied this doctrine with many others foul and odious even to sense, and because they were resisted by Tertullian, a mighty man both in his general abilities and in his particular and professed earnestness to magnify martyrdom. Against these he wrote his *Remedy against a Scorpion's Sting.*

4. This way the orthodox gave no advantage to heretics, who also let loose the bridle of their own nature and seized every occasion of dying as zealously as the orthodox Christians. Because the latter prescribed against them and were ahead of them in numbers, to redeem time and overtake them they constituted new occasions of martyrdom. Petilianus, against whom Saint Augustine wrote, taught that whoever killed himself as a magistrate, to punish a previously committed sin, was a martyr.

There were those whom Saint Augustine and others called Circum-cellians and Circuitores, because (I think, like their master [i.e., the devil], they went about to devour) they would entreat, persuade, and coerce others to kill them. Then, frustrated after all those provocations, they would do it themselves and be celebrated for martyrs by their survivors. These were Donatists, of whom Saint Augustine says, "To kill themselves out of respect for martyrdom was daily sport." Other heretics also, whose errors did not concern martyrdom, hastened to it. So the Cataphrygians who, erroneously baptizing the dead, ordaining women, annulling second marriages, and erring in similar points, could soon boast of their number of martyrs—perhaps because they found Tertullian on their side, since wherever he went he was a hot encourager of men to martyrdom.

Eusebius complained that heretics, seeing their arguments refuted, then fled to their number of martyrs, in which they pretended to exceed the others. From their numbers of martyrs the Euphemites called themselves "martyrians." Baronius says, "Amongst the heathen perchance you may here and there find one Empedocles who will burn himself, but among the Donatists, swarms of men."

5. Thus the authority gained by their zeal to equal the number of true martyrs was so great and began so far to perplex the world that some councils, foreseeing that if both sides did it equally it would all be imputed to human concerns, began to take care to provide against it. One council at Laodicaea exhibits an express canon that no Christian should leave the true martyrs for false ones because they were enemies of God. Another council at Carthage corrects the other heresy of diminishing the reputation of martyrs by directing, "Let nobody who is profane defame the martyrs' dignity."

6. When the true spirit of God drew many, the spirit of contention

drew many also, and other natural infirmities even more, to expose themselves easily to death. It may well be thought that the authors of these later ages have somewhat diminished the intenseness of martyrdom and mingled more alloys, or rather more metal, and made it of not so great value in itself as those earnest times did. Later, Saint Thomas Aquinas said, "Though martyrdom is a work of greatest perfection, yet it is not of itself but only as it is wrought by and expresses charity."

Vázquez reprehends Córdoba for saying that it is any worship of God, for "It is not," says he, "a sacrifice or work of religion but of fortitude, which is only a moral virtue." Navarrus now teaches that "It is a mortal sin to provoke another to inflict martyrdom." It is also taught that a martyr (although martyrdom purges much) is bound to cleanse himself by every one of the degrees of penance, for, says Carbone, "It is not a sacrament but a privileged work." They seem tender and loath by adding religious incitements to cherish or further that desire of dying to which, by reason of our weakness and this world's encumbrances, our nature is too prone and inclined.

Only the Jesuits boast of their seeking martyrdom in the new worlds and of their rage until they find it. Scribanius, who has brought them all upon one scene, says that "Alfonso de Castro at his execution in the Molucca was so overjoyed that he forgot his modesty. 'We snatch martyrdom,' says he, 'with a spontaneous rush.'" Further, "One would think it a disease in us, something we do lest the rest of our life should be devoid of merit and lacking in glory." Again, "We bargain and contract with our profession upon the condition that we squander souls on hostile swords." Yet again, "We possess no more than such small matters as only serve to cut off our life." If this desire of dying is against and not agreeable to the nature of man, apparently it is not against the nature of a Jesuit.

Here we end this discussion, which we intended only for the consideration of this desire of martyrdom that swallowed up all the other inducements which, before Christianity contracted them, tickled and inflamed mankind.

Distinction IV

1. There remains for the fourth and last distinction of this first part only to state the reason by which self-homicide seems to me to escape breaking any law of nature. Both express, literal laws and mute law or custom have authorized it, not only by allowing and conniving in it but also by commissioning it.

It is countenanced not only by many flourishing and well-policed states but also by ideal commonwealths that cunning authors have conceived—in which very enormous faults are unlikely to be allowed. Among the Athenians condemned men were their own executioners by means of poison and among the Romans by means of blood-letting. It is recorded of many places that all sexagenarians were by the laws of wise states thrown from a bridge. Pereira has conjectured that this report was occasioned by a custom in Rome, according to which men of that age were not allowed to vote; since the way to the senate was via a bridge [Latin: *per pontem*], those who by reason of that age were not permitted to come to the senate were called "Depontans."

However that may be, it is more certain that among the Ceans unprofitable old men poisoned themselves; they were crowned with garlands as men triumphant over human misery. The Ethiopians loved death so well that their greatest malefactors, being condemned to banishment, ordinarily escaped it by killing themselves. The civil law, where it appoints no punishment to the delinquent in this case either in his estate or in his memory, punishes a jailer if his prisoner kills himself— out of a prejudice that if the means is afforded them they will all do so.

Do we not see it to be the custom of all nations now to manacle and disarm condemned men, from a prior assurance that otherwise they would escape death by death? Sir Thomas More, a man of the most tender and delicate conscience that the world has seen since Saint Augustine, one who was not likely to write anything in jest or mischievously, says that in Utopia the priests and magistrates used to exhort men afflicted with incurable diseases to kill themselves, and they were obeyed as the interpreters of God's will; but they who killed themselves without giving an account of their reasons to the priests and magistrates were cast out unburied. Plato, who is usually cited against this opinion, disputes it in a fashion as severe and peremptory as this: "What shall we say of him who kills his nearest and dearest friend, who deprives himself of life and of the purpose of destiny?—who, not urged by any sentence or heavy misfortune or exteme shame, but out of a cowardliness and weakness of a fearful mind, unjustly kills himself? What purgatory and what burial by law belongs to him, God himself knows. But let his friends inquire of the interpreters of the law, and do as they shall direct." You see, nothing is said by him against self-homicide except what is said modestly, limitedly, and perplexedly.

This is all that I shall say of the first member of that definition of sin that I undertook, which is transgressing the law of nature. I claim that I have sufficiently delivered and rescued self-homicide from any such violating of the law as may aggravate the act or make it heinous.

THE SECOND PART: OF THE LAW OF REASON

Distinction I

1. The part of the definition of sin that we reserved for the second part is that self-homicide is against the law of reason. If we should interpret reason as rectified reason (especially primarily and originally), it would be the same as the law of nature. I rather choose to admit an interpretation that will bring the most doubts under disputation and therefore into clarity.

Reason, therefore, in this place shall signify conclusions drawn and deduced from the primary reason by our discourse and ratiocination. Thus sin against reason is sin against such arguments and conclusions as by sound consequence may be derived from primary and original reason, which is the light of nature.

This primary reason, against which nobody can plead license, law, custom, or pardon, has in us a sovereign and masculine force. It begets conclusions and resolutions through our discourse, which does the motherly office of shaping, delivering, and rearing them.

2. In earthly kingdoms the king's children and their posterity, as far as we may reasonably presume any tincture of blood, have many privileges and respects due them, which would be forfeited if there appeared any bastardy or interruption of lawful descent from that root. Although the respect and obsequiousness belong to them so far as they are propagated from that root and so far as some sparks of that sovereignty glimmer in them, their servants and officers take them where they find them and consider them only as dukes or lords and possessors of patrimonial estates. Meanwhile, every man's heart is directed and fastened upon the prince, and perhaps a step or two lower with a ready and immediate relation to the father and what they have from him.

Just so! When, from those true propositions that are the eldest children and the issue of our light of nature and of our discourse, conclusions are produced, those conclusions also have the nature of propositions and beget more conclusions. To all these there belongs an assent and submission on our part, if none by the way has been corrupted and bastarded by fallacy. Although, as in the other case, men who are of a weak, lazy, or flattering disposition look no farther into any of these propositions than from whose mouth it proceeds or what authority it now has (not from whence it was produced), still, every man's resolution is fixed upon, arrested by, and submitted to the heir apparent—which is to say, every necessary deduction by natural light. Now human laws, by which kingdoms are policed, are not so very near to this crown of certain truth and first light. If they were necessary consequences from that law of nature, they would not be contrary in various places and times, as we see laws to be. Nevertheless, I justly esteem them nearer and to have more of that royal blood in them than the resolutions of individual men or schools of men.

The first reason is: It is of the essence of all human law that it agrees with nature—I mean obligation in the inner court of conscience. Without this, a law has no more strength than a usurper whom those who obey watch for an opportunity to dispossess.

The second reason is: Assemblies of parliaments, councils, and courts are to be presumed more diligent for delivering and giving birth to those children of natural law. They also give better testimonies than any one man can that no false or suppositious issue is admitted. The law is well called the marriage-contract between the citizens and the republic. That term signifies also that to which they have all betrothed themselves, such as the security and stipulation that the state gives for every man's direction and assurance in all his civil actions. Since in the first part we thoroughly examined whether self-homicide is always of necessity against the law of nature, it is worthy for the first consideration in this second part to inquire how far human laws have determined against it, before we descend to the arguments of particular authors, of whatever reverence or authority.

3. The third reason is: In this disquisition the most general law has the most force and value, and there is no law so general that it deserves the name of the law of nations, or, if there is, it will be the same (as we said before) as rectified reason and thus not differ from the law of nature.

In my understanding, the civil or imperial law once had the greatest extent. Even now it is not being abandoned in its reason, essence, and nature but only lest accepting it should testify some dependence upon the [Holy Roman] Empire. Thus we owe the first place in this consideration to that law.

What do we call the civil law? Properly speaking, the municipal law of every nation is civil law. However, because Rome's emperors deemed the whole world to be one city, as Rome's bishops deem it to be one diocese, the Roman law has won the name of civil law. It is a digest and ordering of all the regal laws, decrees of the senate, plebescites, opinions of experts, and edicts of emperors from 1,400 years before Justinian to as long a time after him as the eastern emperors made them authentic. The civil law is of such largeness that Justinian's part of it consists of 150,000 distinctions (he calls them verses) and is the sum and marrow of many millions, extracted from 2,000 volumes.

This law is so abundant that almost all the points controverted between the Roman and the Reformed Churches may be decided and resolved by it. This law, I say, which has worked upon individuals, fortunes, and consciences both by penalties and anathemas, has pronounced nothing against the self-homicide that we now have under consideration.

It is true that we find one rescript of Hadrian the emperor, who was about 120 years after Christ, in the body of the law: "If a soldier attempts to kill himself and does not accomplish it, unless he tried it under unbearable grief, sickness, sorrow, or some other cause, he shall be capitally punished." This rescript is repeated in another title, and there—although the first general clause or some other cause might seem to have gone far enough—are added especially the excusing causes of "weariness of life, madness, or shame." You see with what moderate gradations this law proceeded. Contending and wrestling (as it seems) with a customary and naturally accomplished act, it does not extend at all to punish self-homicide when it has been done, as the law does in many other crimes by confiscation, by condemning the memory of the delinquent, and by degrading his posterity.

Nor does the rescript embrace all ways of doing it—indeed, hardly any of them, considering how benignly and favorably penal laws are to be interpreted. Nor does it encompass all men, but only those currently in the army, since much disadvantage might befall the army if numbers of them should suddenly be allowed to take this natural, easy way of delivering themselves from painful danger. Just as much damage might befall the state if the enlisted soldiers—to whom there belonged by the laws as many privileges and immunities under the Roman emperors as ever did to the clergy under their Roman bishops—after they had thus maimed themselves and defrauded the state of their service, should by this inherent character of soldiership enjoy all the advantages that the laws afforded them.

One more law in the body of civil law seems to reach farther, because it does not bind itself to any one condition of men; that is, "If a man who, already accused or caught in the act of any crime for which his goods would be forfeited upon conviction, should kill himself before judgment, his goods shall be forfeited." Or it may *not* reach farther, for the law adds this opinion of the act: "It is not the deed's evil that is liable to punishment but the guilt of conscience." It goes on, "He who has reason to die may have an heir." Thus the law presumes that there *are* just causes to work this effect.

Upon the consideration of this civil law I determined to bestow this first distinction.

Distinction II

1. What they call the canon law is of even larger extent than the civil, for it reaches to bind the princes themselves, at least by their

acceptance of and submission to it. As its subject is greater, being people and princes, so is its object, being the next or eternal life. Indeed, it is so vast and unbounded that we do not know in what books to seek its limits nor by what rules to set the landmarks of its jurisdiction.

As for the book, it is evident that the primitive church had canonical codes, which were inserted into the body of the Roman law and had no other existence except as it was incorporated there. Thus Gelasius wrote to Theodoric the Gothic king of Italy, pleading that, just as by his authority the Roman law was observed in civil matters, so it might be the same in ecclesiastical matters. After the expulsion of the Goths, Leo IV pleaded for and obtained the same from Lothair I. From this canonical code the emperors decided and decreed in many ecclesiastical causes. From this code the subsequent councils were governed in making their canons; we may see particular canons of this book cited—the book often called for in councils and commonly named, the Body of the Canon Law. This body consisted of the canons of nine councils authorized by the emperors.

There have been immense additions to it since that time—bulls and decretal letters of popes; decrees of suspicious, partial, and schismatic councils (for nothing is more properly schism and a breach of succession than a rent between the civil and ecclesiastical state, which occasioned many of the later councils); the rags of Fathers excerpted and digested by Gratian plus the glosses on these that became as authentic as the text. I do not see what all these additions have to do with the Body of Canon Law, except where princes have incorporated and naturalized them.

However, since for us to quarrel now with their authority may seem a subterfuge and a shift to turn away from them as though they were heavily against us in the matter at hand, we shall accept them as they are set forth and disguise nothing in them that seems to resist our opinion. In the common usage this law is likely to be severe against self-homicide. The civil laws always content themselves with any excuse or color in favor of the delinquents, because when a fault is proved it is punished severely. But canon laws, which punish only medicinally and for the soul's health, are apt to presume or believe guiltiness on light evidence, because their punishments always work good effects, whether or not they are just.

2. Because heresy, which is treason against divine majesty, is of all crimes the principal object of that court, I say there is nothing at all heretical about self-homicide, according to anything extant in the canon law. This is true, even allowing the widest definition of heresy, which (according to Simancas) is, "Anything against catholic faith; that is, scriptures rightly understood, or the traditions and definitions of the church or general councils lawfully gathered, or definition of the apostolic see, or the common opinion of the Fathers, in a matter of faith."

Self-homicide may perhaps to some seem possessed of bad qualities. It may be ill-sounding, audacious, or perhaps discreet heresy. But all of these proceed from the indisposition and distempered taste of the accuser, who must not always be idly flattered and pampered but invited to the search and discovery of truth; otherwise, the accuser, even if he is the greatest prince in the world, would have no access to his realm but be cramped in a wretched corner.

We may cast a glance upon each part of the definition of heresy. The question whether or not self-homicide is against the scriptures rightly understood will be more properly and naturally examined when we come to the last part of this essay, concerning divine law. Next, there is no tradition or definition at all by the church on self-homicide, much less as a matter of faith, which is the second limb of the definition. There is no decree by any general council. There is no rescript or bull by any pope.

What about the common opinion of the Fathers? We lay aside the fact that this cannot be a safe rule because, as Azorius notes, "Controverters on both sides often say that theirs is the common opinion, and certainly what is the common opinion in one age is not that in another. Indeed, what is common opinion in one kingdom at the same time is not that in another kingdom, although both are Catholic. In Germany and France by common opinion adoration is not due to the cross but in Spain by common opinion it is." It cannot appear from the canon law that there is a common opinion of the Fathers against self-homicide. Gratian, who alone of the compilers of canon law, as far as either my reading or search has discovered, touches the point, cites only two Fathers, Augustine and Jerome, and the latter is of the opinion that there may be some cause to do it. But in the canon law I find no words either to lay upon it the infamous name of heresy, or to label it with the mark or style of sin, or to condemn the deed by inflicting any punishment on the offender!

I speak here of that canon law with which the canonists deal, the decretal letters and all the extravagants [i.e., the originally uncodified decretals]. That learned and ingenious bishop of Tarragon, Antonio Agustín, has taught us what we should think of Gratian's *Decretal*. He says, "He is hardly worth much reprehension who, having nothing that is profitable or of use unless he borrows it, is admired by the ignorant and laughed at by the learned, who never saw the books of the council, nor the works of the Fathers, nor the registers of the pope's letters, and whose compilation lacked the confirmation by Eugenius III that is falsely attributed to it." At any rate, Gratian does not have so much authority that by his inserting an imperial law or fragment of a Father it should therefore be canonized and grafted into the body and force of canon law. For then, even if that law was abrogated by the emperor, it would still be alive and bind by a stronger obligation in the canon, which Alberigo Gentili proves to be against the common opinion! Still, by consent this much is afforded

Gratian, that texts cited by him have as much authority in him as they had in the author from whom he took them. Therefore, when we come to handle in their proper place the reasons of particular authors, we omit none whom Gratian has cited.

3. In this distinction we handle the opinion of the canon law on self-homicide, not because Gratian cites it but because the canons of all councils are now appropriated as canon law. So we shall consider a canon he cites from the Councils of Braga.

First, although he does not cite it, we shall not conceal the Council of Auxerre, which was held (before the other) under Gregory the Great in the year 590. The civil laws, by limitation of persons and causes, gave some restraint and correction to this natural desire to die when we wish. They did so out of a need to sinew and strengthen as far as they were able the doctrine of our blessed savior, who, having ended all bloody sacrifices, enlightens us with another doctrine, that to endure the miseries and afflictions of this life is wholesome and advantageous to us. The Councils, also perceiving that this first engrafted and inborn desire needed all possible restraints, contributed their help.

This canon, then, has these words, "If any kill themselves, oblations in that instance shall not be received." It seems that preaching and catechizing had wrestled and fought with the Christian's natural appetite and tamed them to perplexity as to whether or not it might be done. Thinking to make sure work in an indiscreet devotion, they gave oblations to the church to expiate the fault—if there were any. The Council forbids receiving these oblations. However, it decrees nothing on the point as a matter of faith, only providing against an inconvenient practice. What it decreed was not very obligatory or considerable, since it was only a diocesan council of one bishop and his abbots, one whose canons Binius presents because, he says, although some of them are out of use (of which this may be one), they tell us something about antiquity.

The other council that Gratian cites—and besides these two I find none—has these words, "For those who kill themselves there shall be no commemoration at the oblation, nor shall they be brought to burial with psalms." This intimates, as the language of the canon law has it, a dog's burial.

But the gloss on this borrows from another canon, that if the person was not under excommunication, it is of no effect, "For we may communicate with him dead with whom we may communicate living." This shows that his act of dying in this way put him into no worse state in this respect. This answers the first punishment inflicted by that canon.

As for the second, which is denial of Christian burial, it is very severe to conclude from that the heinousness of the act, since the true canon law denies Christian burial to men slain at a tilting, even though it affords them, if they are not already dead, all the sacraments applicable in that extremity—penance, eucharist, and unction. Although this gloss denies burial to men whom they deem in a state and way of salvation, it gathers reasonably that "This punishment does not reach to the dead but works only to deter the living," referring to this purpose an epistle of Gregory the Great that says, "So much as a sumptuous funeral profits a wicked man, just so much a base funeral or none at all harms a godly man."

Last, there is the Clementine canon that lists many causes for which Christian burial is denied. One of them is a local interdict concerning the time when the holiest man who dies in some place cannot be buried, and the rule sometimes extends to whole kingdoms! This canon instructs us sufficiently that one may be subject to such punishment (if it is in any law) and still not be guilty of such a crime as this one is reputed to be.

The Romans in their religious discipline refused solemn burial to any who perished by lightnings. However, they buried offenders in the town, as they did vestals and emperors, since their dedication to God had delivered the nuns and their sovereignty had delivered the emperors from the bondage of law. So did justice, to which they had made full satisfaction, deliver punished offenders. Since both Saint Jerome and the Councils of Braga inflict upon those catechumens who, although they had all other preparations and degrees of maturity in the Christian faith, departed this world without baptism, the same punishments as they do upon self-murderers, making them equal in punishment and consequently in guiltiness, I think it ill becomes the doctrines of our times and the analogy to pronounce so desperately the damnation either of the unbaptized or of self-homicides.

Here we end our second distinction of this second part, which was allotted to the examination of the canon law.

Distinction III

1. Among arguments that are conclusions deduced out of reason and discourse, after these general laws of the empire and of the church I may justly rank the laws of particular states. (Those of the church might seem to merit first consideration by virtue of their generality; we handled them second because their power has always been litigious and questionable).

According to our English law, therefore, he who kills himself is reckoned as one who commits a felony against himself. This law has not been long in practice, for Bracton seems not to know it; in an entire chapter on the title he only repeats the words in the imperial law that I cited before and so acknowledges that if he admitted that law he would admit the exception, without just cause. Whether or not this felon against himself is chargeable with any offense, he forfeits his goods. These goods, devolving to the king's almoner, are to be employed on the king's behalf in pious and charitable uses. According to this law, the deed is not only homicide but also murder. But the reasons alleged are only that the king has lost a subject, that his peace is broken, and that it is an evil example.

In my understanding, this law has no foundation in natural or imperial law, nor does it receive much force from those three reasons, having by custom alone put on the nature of law, as most of our law has. I believe it was first introduced among us because we were excessive in the natural desire of dying in this way. What has led us back from it is not a better understanding of nature but the wisdom of lawmakers and observers of things fit for the institution and conservation of states.

In ancient commonwealths the numbers of slaves were infinite. Both in Rome and in Athens there were always ten slaves for every citizen. Pliny says that in Augustus's time Isidorus had more than 4,000 and Vedius Pollio so many that he always fed his fish in ponds with their blood. Since such servitude has eroded, the number of wretched men still exceeds the happy, for every laborer is miserable and beastlike compared to the idle, abounding men. It was therefore thought necessary by laws and by the opinions of religion—as Scaevola is alleged to have said, "One expects states to be deceived about religion"—to take from these weary and mascerated wretches their ordinary and open escape and ease, voluntary death.

Therefore, self-homicide, like hunting and usury, seems to be prohibited, as a lawyer says, "Lest men be enticed." Thus, to withdraw his nation from wine Muhammad brought them to a religious belief that in every grape there was a devil.

What among us is a natural disease, stealing—for like all others this vice may abound in a nation as well as in a particular man, and Dorotheus relates at length the sickness of one of his friars who could not abstain from stealing, although he had no use for what he stole—has drawn from a Council held at London under Henry III a canon that excommunicates the harborers of thieves, "Who thereby abound in the kingdom of England." The canon mentions no fault except this one. And from custom, princes, and parliaments come severer laws against theft than are justifiable by nature or by the Jews' judicial law (Exod. 22:1). For our law hangs a man for stealing in extreme necessity, even though such necessity brings him to consider all things as originally belonging to the community, and even though he is bound in conscience to steal and, according to some opinions, would be a self-murderer if he did not steal.

Duns Scotus, disputing against the laws of those nations that allow the death of a thief who robs by day, because whoever kills such a thief is expressly by God's law a murderer, asks, Where have you read of excepting such a thief from the law, "You shall not kill" (Exod. 20:13)? Or where have you seen a [papal] bull fallen from heaven to justify such executions? It may be that a natural leaning in our people to such a manner of death weakened the state and might have occasioned severer laws than the common ground of all laws seems to support.

Therefore, when the emperor made a law to stop a common abuse of impious men, decreeing that no man might give anything to the clergy, not even by bequest, Saint Jerome said, "I lament and grieve, not that such a law is made, but that our manners have deserved such a law." Just so, in contemplating these laws, I mourn that the infirmity and sickness of our nation needs such medicines.

The same must be said of a similar law in the earldom of Flanders. If it is true that they allow the confiscation of goods in only five cases, of which self-homicide is one, thus ranking it with treason, heresy, sedition, and deserting the army against the Turk, then these are strong and urgent circumstances to reduce this desire in men.

2. Where you find many severe laws against an offense, you do not safely conclude an extreme enormity or heinousness in the fault. You safely infer a propensity of that people at that time to that fault. For this reason, Ignatius and many others—even entire councils—were forced to pronounce that those who fasted on Sundays were murderers of Christ. So in France the laws abound against duels, to which they are head-longly apt. So the resolutions of the Spanish casuists and the bulls of the popes are repeated and exaggerated in that nation against bull-fighting, to which they are so enormously addicted. Still, of itself bull-fighting is no sin, as Navarrus, retracting his opinion after seventy years, at last holds.

These severe laws no more increase a fault than mild punishments diminish it. No man thinks rape a small fault, although Solon punishes it, if the victim is a virgin and free-born, with money that would amount to our five shillings. The Salic Law punishes pecuniarily and at no high price a witch convicted of having eaten a man. Therefore, Bartolus allows that, in cases of public profit or detriment, the judges may extend an odious and burdensome law beyond the letter and restrain a favorable and beneficial law within it, even though this is against the nature and common practice of both these laws.

If, therefore, our law and the Flemish law are severe in punishing self-homicide, and if this argument has more force because more nations concur in such laws, it may well be answered that everywhere men are inclinable to it. This goes far to establish our opinion, considering that none of those laws that prescribe civil restraints from doing it can make it sin. The act is not much discredited if it is evil only because it is so forbidden and if it binds the conscience only to the general precept of obedience to the law or to the forfeiture of goods.

3. It seems from the practice of the Jews (for Josephus speaks of it as a usual thing) that they did not bury until the sun set those who killed

themselves. I do not know upon what law of theirs they grounded this, and I do not find out from writers about their policies since the dispersion. (They have no magistracy but live under the laws of the places into which they are admitted, in all cases except where they are exempted by privilege.) Still, they do testify to a particular detesting of some sins by public penances among themselves. For theft they bind, whip, and enjoin to public confession, and for adultery the offender sits naked for a day—in winter in freezing water and in summer on an anthill or among hives of bees. Although I do not find from Galatino, Sigonio, Buxtorf, or Molther that self-homicide was or is usual among them, still, because Josephus says it (although only oratorically), we shall accept it and believe that it was done for the reason common to almost all nations, to deter men from doing it and not to punish its being done. Of similar use—that is, in deterrence—was the law of the Athenians, who after death cut off the hand that perpetrated that deed, which law Josephus remembers in the same place.

4. The reason that is grounded upon the edict of Tarquinius Priscus proves no more than the above. When this desire of death reigned among his men like a contagion, he cured it by an opprobrious hanging up of their bodies and exposing them to birds and beasts. The same holds for the way of restraining the Virgins of Miletus. When they had a wantoness of dying thus and did it for fashion, they were by decree dishonorably exhibited naked as a spectacle to the people. Neither case prevails farther than the previous argument. Each proves only a watchful solicitude in every state by all means to avert men from this natural love of ease, by which their strength in numbers would have been very much impaired.

So we end this distinction.

Distinction IV

We will now proceed to those reasons that particular men have used for detesting this action. First, we will pay our debt to Gratian by considering the texts he cited. Afterwards in this distinction, the other reasons of authors who were theologians (unless they are grounded in verses of scripture, which we postpone for the last part) shall have their ventilation.

1. The first text is an epistle of Saint Augustine to Donatus the heretic, who, having been apprehended by the Catholics, fell from his horse and would have drowned himself. He afterward complained of violence used toward him in matters of religion, wherein he claims freedom of election and conscience. Saint Augustine answers that we have the power to try to save our souls against our wills, as it is lawful for us thus to save our bodies. If you were constrained to do evil, even so you ought not kill yourself. Consider whether in the scriptures you find any of the faithful

who did so when they suffered much from those who would have forced them to do things to their souls' destruction.

I shall speak a little of Saint Augustine in general, because almost all the reasons of others are derived from him. He was writing purposely about self-homicide from the seventeenth to the twenty-seventh chapters of the first book of *On the City of God*. Now the writers on confession in our times, comparing Navarrus and Soto, two of the greatest casuists, decide sometimes that Navarrus is sounder and more learned but Soto more useful and applicable to practical divinity. Just so, I say that for sharp insight and conclusive judgment in exposition of places of scripture, which he always makes so liquid and pervious, Saint Augustine has hardly been equaled by any of all the writers in the church of God. (Except that Calvin may have that honor, and where it does not concern points in controversy I see the Jesuits themselves often follow him; although they dare not name him, they pay him high respect and reverence.)

In practical learning and moral divinity Saint Augustine was so fastidious, refined, and rigorous a conscience—perhaps to redeem his former licentiousness, for such converts often happen to be extremely zealous—that for our direction in the conduct of this life, Saint Jerome and some others may be thought sometimes fitter to adhere to than Saint Augustine. But I do not say this as though we needed this medicament for this text. For I agree with Saint Augustine that neither to avoid occasion of sin nor for any other cause wherein I myself am merely or principally interested may I do this act, which also serves justly for an answer to the same zealous Father in the other text cited by Gratian. For with him I confess that "He who kills himself is so much the more guilty therein as he was guiltless of the fact for which he killed himself."

Nevertheless, by the way, this principle may not pass generally without admitting the exception carried by the rule of law on which it is grounded, "No one without guilt ought to be punished unless there is an offsetting cause." And so, like Saint Augustine, we may say with as much earnestness, "This we assert, this we say, this we approve in every respect, that neither to avoid temporal trouble, nor to remove from others the occasion to sin, nor to punish our own past sins, nor to prevent future sins, nor out of desire for the next life, where these are the only or the principal considerations, can it be lawful for any man to kill himself." But neither Saint Augustine nor we deny that, if there are cases where the party is disinterested and the glory of God is only or primarily respected and advanced, self-homicide may be lawful.

Valens the emperor surprised Iamblicus when his divining cock had described three letters of the name of the person who would succeed him and slew all whose names were Theodorus, Theodotes, or Theodulus, but he let off Theodosius, who fulfilled the prophecy. In the same way, Saint Augustine has condemned those causes that we do not defend and has omitted those in which it is justifiable.

This case is hard to discern and distinguish from others arising from human infirmity. If the rule that Antonio de Córdoba gives in cases of simony is, as he says it is, a good guide in all perplexities, it will help very much. He says that in the case of simony many difficulties arise, since not only (by clear and common judgments) temporal reward may be taken for spiritual offices by way of gifts, stipends, wages, alms, sustenance, or fulfilling the law or custom of a place, but also according to some doctors even by way of price and bargain, if not directly for the spiritual part thereof then for the labor necessarily attached to it. Since not every curate can distinguish in these cares, he bids them, "Always do it with an intention to do it as God knows it may be done and as wise men know and would teach that it might be done. For, humbly remitting ourselves to instruction by the learned who are our fathers, whatever defect may be in us, let us be saved by the parents' faith." In this way Pindar, making an implicit prayer to God that he would give him what he knew to be best for him, died in that very petition.

Since Saint Augustine has in his decision the qualification that a better life never receives a man after a death of which he himself was guilty, we will be as bold with him as one who is more obliged to him than we. Thyraeus, repeating Augustine's opinion that the devil could not possess a body unless he entered into it by sin, rejects the opinion and says, "The holy Father speaks not of what must of necessity be, but of what for the most part actually is."

2. In our case I think we ought to follow Saint Jerome's temper. In his exposition of the book of Jonah (I wonder why Gratian cited it, being so far from his aim and advantage) he says, "In persecution I may not kill myself unless [original: without this, where] chastity is endangered." Here I am far from agreeing with Gratian that "'without this' is inclusively spoken and amounts to the phrase, 'not even if' [original: no not though]," for I think that good and learned Father, Jerome, included in the word "chastity" all purity of religion and manners, and to a man so rectified death comes always and in every way seasonably and welcome. For "As death finds a man, so a man finds death."

3. From this text Saint Jerome, I believe, and some others whom I perhaps have not read, and from some other texts in others, charitably dissent. Lavater, having profited from all of Peter Martyr's reasons mostly against self-homicide and adding some of his own when they both handle the duties of Saul, confesses that in this case of preserving chastity Augustine, Chrysostom, Lactantius, and Jerome departed from the opinion of those who condemned this act.

4. Peter Martyr also presents one other reason of which he seems glad and well contented; namely, that we must not hasten death because death is an evil. But this reason is not worthy of his gravity, especially so

long after Clement of Alexandria had so thoroughly defeated that opinion. For even if it is an evil, it is only an evil of punishment, and that is an evil of which God is the author. It is not that evil by which we are evil, neither does it always prove the patient to be evil (although God for all that is always just), for Christ himself said of the man born blind, "Neither he nor his parents have sinned" (John 9:5).

Concerning that evil of punishment, which is deemed the greatest of temporal afflictions in this life because of the close danger of impairing our soul (that is, to be possessed), Thyraeus, drawing on Saint Jerome and Chrysostom, says that it is not always inflicted only for sin but also to manifest the glory of God. The greatest evil of this kind that can be imagined, which is "Damnation, has less of the essence of evil than has the least sin that brings us damnation," says Aquinas. Death is therefore an act of God's justice, and when he is pleased to inflict it he may choose his officer and choose me myself as well as anybody else.

Even if it were the worst sort of evil, still, as Saint Augustine says, "In the act of marriage there is a good use of evil, that is of concupiscence, which is an evil adulterers evilly use." The good Paulinus praises Sulpicius Severus because "He, having the liberty of sinning in marriage, did not depart from his accustomed austerity." The same may be said of death in some cases, as in martyrdom.

Although Peter Martyr urges further that death is called God's "enemy" (I Cor. 15:26) and is therefore evil, Musculus says about that text, "Death is often commended in scripture because God uses it for the faithful to good ends and makes it work toward salvation." By what authority can they so assuredly pronounce that it happens in our case of self-homicide? Besides, death has already lost much of its natural malignity and is not now so evil as it naturally was at first. Calvin notes, "It is already so destroyed that it is not lethal but only grievous."

5. Peter Martyr offers another reason of his own, that life is a gift, and because it is the gift of God it may not be refused. When we have agreed with him that it may not be unthriftily and prodigally cast away, how can he conclude from self-homicide such an ingratitude as that I shall forsake God's glory? May I in no case lay down my life? How can "I may never" follow from "I must not always"?

6. Lavater, following many others, urges that because judges are established for the purpose, no man should take dominion over himself. But in the Church of England, where auricular confession is neither under precept nor much in practice (the idea that we do not allow it at all or reject it as the Waldenses did, although a reverend man said it, is more than I ever knew), who is the judge of sin, against which no civil law provides or of which there is no evidence? May not I accuse and condemn myself to myself and inflict what penance I will to punish the past, avoiding similar occasion of sin?

Upon this reason turns that perplexed question of whether the pope may not give himself absolution from acts and vows, and partake of his own indulgences. By the best opinions it is agreed that to do so is an act of jurisdiction, which by Lavater's rule no man may exercise upon himself. The imperial laws generally forbid anybody to be judge in his own cause, but all the commentators make an exception of sovereigns. Concerning ordinary judges, all agree with Baldus that "In a notorious deed if the dignity of the judge is concerned, he is the proper judge of it." He also says, "It belongs to the chief magistrate to judge whether or not such a cause belongs under his judgment." With a "notwithstanding" to natural law, as the words of the privilege have it, Theodoric allowed bishops to be judges in their own cause. So "If a son who had not been judge in his own cause, had been made consul, he might have emancipated himself or authorized another to have adopted him."

Moreover, it appears that the popes have exercised jurisdiction upon themselves, even before they were popes. John XXII, having permission to choose one pope, chose himself, which deed Nauclerus relates and justifies. According to canonical rules, it is plain that he may exercise jurisdiction upon himself in any case where there is not a distinction of persons enjoined by the law of God, as in baptism—which will not be stretched in our case.

Certainly the reason for the law that none should be judge in his own cause is that everyone is presumed to favor himself. Therefore, if the law is dispensable in some cases that are beneficial to a man, much more may it be so in cases of inflicting punishment, in which nobody is imagined to be overly strict on himself. Even if man were by nature as slavish as the "Essenes were by profession and rule, who had power over themselves only in serving and being compassionate," except when self-homicide becomes an act of advantage to ourselves, we have enough jurisdiction to do it. It is more certainly proved that in some cases derogatory and prejudicial to us we have this right over ourselves, that every man may become judge in his own cause and not exercise the privilege.

Everybody condemned Gregory XII in the Great Schism when, after he had promised to depart from the papacy by an oath in which there was a clause that he should neither ask, give, nor accept absolution from that oath, he induced his mendicants to preach that it would be a mortal sin for him utterly to relinquish power over the church. Many kings at their own pleasure have departed from their governments and relieved themselves of their burdens. What one says of the whole church may be said of every particular member, "It was always in political bondage but not in spiritual bondage."

If there are cases in which one may—assuredly or probably, after just diligence has been used—decide to do something because of an illumination from the spirit of God or from a ceasing of the reason of the law at that time in him, that man is then judge in his own cause.

Although in cases where there is a proper court I am bound by it, yet as two kings who are both sovereigns may justly decide a cause by war because there can be no competent judge between them, just so, in secret cases between the spirit of God and my conscience of which there is no certainly constituted, exterior judge, we are ourselves sufficient to do all the offices. Then, delivered from all bondage and restored to our natural liberty, we are in the same condition as princes. If in the strictest sense they may not properly be said to give themselves privileges, still they have one general, inherent privilege, for, when they will, they may declare that in that particular case they will not take a new privilege but exercise their old one.

7. Because Josephus has one reason that smacks of theology, we will consider it here. He says our soul is a small part of God, deposited and committed in trust to us, and we may not neglect or dislodge it before God withdraws it. We are still on safe ground in saying that whenever I may justly depart this life it is by a summons from God, and it cannot then be imputed to any corruption of my will. For "He who yields to authority is believed not to exercise his will." I expect there was never a particular inspiration or a new commission, such as they are forced to purchase for Samson and the rest of the self-homicides, except from that resident and inherent grace of God by which he excites us to works of moral or higher virtues.

Therefore, when anything for which we are the depositaries is called for again, is would be a greater injustice in us to deny or withhold it than if we were debtors—just so, not to depart from Josephus's allusion or metaphor of a deposit. If it was a fault to let go that of which I am depositary before it was truly called for, still with an erring conscience I would be excusable, for it is "Of the essence of a deposit that the depositary is held for what is lost by deceit, not by fault," according to Soto. Indeed, when I have a secret from another, given in trust, in all respects I hold it in the nature of a deposit, and yet nobody doubts that in many cases I may share this secret.

8. Many metaphorical and allegorical reasons scattered among authors, as in Cicero and Macrobius, were made more for illustration than for argument or answer. I will not stand to glean among them, since they are almost all bound up in one sheaf in that oration of Josephus, or else will be fitly handled in those texts of scripture that make such allusions.

9. In that oration Josephus gives one reason drawn from the way we deal with enemies. We count them enemies who make attempts on our lives. Shall we be enemies to ourselves? Since in this text Josephus speaks to save his own life, he may justly be thought to speak more sincerely and dispassionately. Where in the person of Eleazar he persuades people

to kill themselves, there is neither certain truth in the assertion nor in the consequence. But do we count God or the magistrate our enemy when death is inflicted by them? Do not martyrs, in whose death God is glorified, kiss their executioners and the instruments of their death? Is it unlawful, unnatural, or inexpedient for us in many cases to be our own enemies when we deny ourselves many things agreeable to our sensitive nature and inflict upon ourselves many things repugnant to that nature? This was abundantly shown in the first part.

10. In the same oration Josephus has another allusory argument: "A servant who runs away is to be punished by the law, even if his master is severe; much more, if we run away from so indulgent a master as God is to us." Not to give strength or delight to this reason by affording a long or diligent answer, we say that in self-homicide the servant runs not *from* his master but *to* him and at his call obeys his voice. Still, it is as truly as it is devoutly said, "The devil is overcome by resisting, but the world and the flesh by running away." And the farther the better!

11. His last point that is of any taste is, "In a tempest it is the part of an idle and treacherous pilot to sink the ship." But I say that if in a tempest we must cast the most precious ware overboard to save the lives of the passengers, and the merchant who suffers loss thereby cannot impute this to anybody or remedy it himself, how much more may I, when I am weather-beaten and in danger of betraying the precious soul that God has embarked in me, put off this burdensome flesh until it becomes his pleasure that I shall resume it? This is not to sink the ship but to retire it to safe harbor and assured anchor.

Thus our fourth distinction, which was to embrace the reasons proposed by particular authors, whether sacred or profane, oblique and metaphorical as well as direct, shall here be ended.

Distinction V

1. Another sort of reason is produced from the grounds of the moral virtues, of which Saint Thomas Aquinas proposes two that we delimit for this distinction. Saint Augustine's reason, that it is against fortitude, has another bearing. Aquinas says it is against justice and against charity.

As to the reason that it is against justice, there are two aspects. The first is that the self-homicide steals a person and member of the body from the universe or from the state to which his service is due. The second is that he usurps the right of God.

The first may as well be said of all who, withdrawing themselves from functions in the commonwealth, defraud the state of their assistance and attend only to their own ends, whether in this life or the next. Certainly to do even that so intently that we neglect our office in society is the same offense in kind as this one. Although many follow Aquinas here, Navarro, Sayer, and others have a better reason for the opinion that this cannot be a sin against justice.

As for the second reason, I say it does not usurp God's authority or deal with another's servant if I become God's servant, delegate, and commissioner in self-homicide, when in no other way he can be so much glorified. Surely the passage from this life to the next is not generally left to our free will, and nobody is properly lord of his own life. Still, according to Sayer, "Although we do not have the dominion, we do have the use of this life, and it is lawful for us to lose that use when we will." How little and narrow a distance there is between negative and positive killing and how contiguous they are, we shall see in another place. If, therefore, the reason why we may not die by self-homicide is because we are not lords of our own life but God alone is lord of it, then the state cannot take away our life, for "It is no more lord of our life than we are," says Sayer; that is, the state cannot do it except in cases where it is God's officer.

If by self-homicide any injury were done to the state, then certainly it would be in the power of the state to license a man to do it, and with such license he would be excusable in conscience. For the state to do so would be only to cede its own right, which anybody may lawfully do. Finally, if the state were injured by self-homicide, the state might lawfully recover its damage from the heirs and goods of the delinquent. However, except in those places where express laws allow it, this cannot be done. I think the better opinion, to judge by the number of authors, is that if the person is of necessary use to that state, there are in self-homicide some degrees of injustice, but no more than if a general of much use should retire into a monastery.

If we could safely take the decision that self-homicide is not against justice, we would ease ourselves of all the labor that must be spent on the third part. Since the foundation of that part will be principally the commandment, "You shall not kill" (Exod. 20:13), if this killing is not against justice, it breaks no part of the Decalogue and thus is not a sin.

Should any consider self-homicide an injustice to ourselves, Aquinas in the same text clears that up. Were it possible for a man to injure himself, which it is not, this injury might oftentimes be such as Cicero says of his banishment, "In no way an expelling, but an improving," considering how much happiness might recompense it.

Because charity is not properly a moral virtue, and because many of the scriptural texts that we must handle in the last part are built on this ground of charity, we will not examine whether or not it is against charity until we come to that part. Here I will only say that, although it is still under dispute and questionable whether or not self-homicide is against charity, it is certainly against charity to pronounce so desperately against those who fall into it as men are used to doing.

2. Aristotle suggests two reasons that are derived from the rules of moral virtue. Observing that this kind of death caught men by two baits, ease and honor, against those who die to avoid misery he teaches that death is the greatest misery that can befall us. Leaving aside the question of how it can agree with the rest of his doctrine, for its purpose this was the most slippery and devious argument. Then, so that honor and fame might draw none to it, he says, "It is cowardliness and dejection, and the argument of a tender and impatient mind."

We have already spoken about the first charge in answer to one of Peter Martyr's reasons. About the other one we shall have occasion to say enough when we come to a place where Saint Augustine says the same thing. Therefore, we may relieve this distinction of that business.

Distinction VI

1. Having considered the reasons that are found in the best authors, and having shown such rules as serve for the true understanding of them and of all others that spring from the same or similar topics, before we terminate this second part concerning the law of reason, we must also touch those reasons in *favor* of our side that others have produced and that we may produce. According to these, self-homicide may be affirmed either wholly or in part.

I shall not stop long upon the law and practice in Rome, that anybody who had his causes approved by the Senate might kill himself. About this Quintilian frames a case. A son, who by astrologers' predictions was to kill first many enemies and then his father, having in the wars performed the first part makes petition to the Senate that before he comes to perform the last part he be allowed to kill himself. Quintilian argues for the son, with many reasons applicable to his particular case and to our main question. But I shall hasten to our chief strength.

2. It will shed much light on this business if we compare desertion with destruction and consider where and how they differ. Certainly, in Almighty God it is not the same thing to forsake and to destroy, because he owes us nothing and always in his forsakings there are degrees of mercy, since he might justly destroy us and then afterwards at his good pleasure return again to us.

It is otherwise between men who are mutual debtors and naturally bound to one another, for a magistrate or minister who abandons his charge and neglects it destroys it. So says Agapetus the Deacon to Justinian the emperor, "For subjects commission but for princes omission is a vice." Indeed, a private man who does not but could and should hinder a man's wrong performs the fault. "If you have not fed one who is dying of hunger, you have slain him," says Ambrose. Also, "That clergyman who does not hinder a manslaughter if he can is thereby suspended." He who denies himself necessary things or exposes himself inordinately to dangers that men usually do not escape kills himself. He who is as sure that this medicine will cure him as that this poison will destroy him is as guilty if he refuses the medicine as he is if he swallows the poison. For which is less dangerous, to attend the collapsing of a house, the flooding of a stream, or the incursion of mad beasts? Those who compare omissions with commissions ask no more to make them equal than that we omit something that we could and should do!

3. Concerning such faults as are greatest, either in their own nature or in their being beyond remedy once they are done, all laws say that every approach, even the very first step, to them carries the same guilt and is under the same punishment as the fault itself. In treason and heresy the first consent is the absolute fault. We have an example of a woman who was burned for petty treason for contriving the death of her husband, although it was not done.

Homicide is one of these crying sins that has always been reckoned among atrocities. Although the Athenians repealed by disuse all of Draco's laws because of their extreme severity, they retained those against homicide. Homicide, says Toledo, may be done five ways: by commandment, by advice, by permission, by help, or by the act itself. In the first and worst homicide, committed in Paradise, in which were employed all the persons in the world who were able to concur in evil—although there was only one man, all the millions who ever have been and ever will be were massacred at once, and himself too—as many of these kinds of homicides were found as was possible in so few persons. Reuchlin notes, "The serpent counseled, the woman helped, and Adam perpetrated" the first sin—and, we may safely say, God permitted it! If every one of these acts is a kind of homicide, no approach towards it can be lawful, if any is itself lawful, that is not homicide. Let us therefore consider how far and in how many of these ways self-homicide may be allowable.

4. First, although the commonly received opinion is that "The one who instigates a crime and the one who perpetrates it are subject to the same punishment," we cannot properly apply the precept to ourselves, because in this act the same party must be the agent, the patient, and the instrument.

We may come close but not properly to the nature of it by the second way of advice, so that after discourse we may advisedly choose one of these roles and refuse the others, for whoever can be willing can also be unwilling. So we may wish for ourselves what is naturally evil (I mean the evil of punishment); the hermit monk, according to Sulpicius Severus, by earnest prayer obtained from God permission to be possessed by the devil for certain months, because he found in himself an inclination to pride and security.

Certainly in some cases we may without sinning wish for death, and not only for enjoying the sight of God—so says a holy man, "For a vision of God, we long a thousand times to consign our body to death"—but also to be delivered from the encumbrances of this life. So the act can have good reasons, as Peter Martyr argues, and then says, "To refuse the better deed is corruption of the first condition." Thus we may wish for death, even though it is so far from being lawful to wish anything that "It is sin to wish that anything naturally evil were not evil, so that we might then wish it when it was discharged of that natural evilness." Death itself, therefore, is not evil, nor is it evil to wish for it. Is it then evil to further with more actual help that which we may lawfully wish to be done?

The two extreme religions that seem to degrade secular magistracy by subjecting monarchs either to a bishop or to a consistory willingly accept this saying, "Curse not the king, no not in your heart" (Eccl. 10:20); that is, do not wish him ill. Nor, as I observe, have the authors of either persuasion allowed in their books that the subject might wish the death of the prince except in cases where he might contribute his actual help. For both Papists and Puritans teach that a lawful king may become a tyrant, which in my understanding cannot consist with the form and right of hereditary monarchy. Still, Saravia, who pretends to go the middle way—in this case, truly the royal way—says, "We as well as the Romanists deem a king of another religion to be a tyrant" and, "It is impossible to make one a king without his being a tyrant in the opinion of one side or the other." As for his own opinion, he writes, "No man can be bound by an oath of fidelity to the pope, because he is not indeed the vicar of God as he presumed and swore himself to be."

Conformably with this view, that book whose title and scope is the foundation of matters of state in France (and, it pretends, in all Christendom), *Declaration et Protestation des Doctes de France*, after it has enraged subjects against tyrants and comes to declare what a tyrant is, exemplifies it in the king of Spain, and with reasons that cast whatever malignity the author is equal to upon whatever prince he chooses.

Last, whoever will compare carefully Beccaria's book with Beza's (if that other book is Beza's) will see that, although they differ diametrically in many things, still from their collision and beating together there arise abundantly the sparks of this pestilent doctrine, that as tranquility once was so religion now is the reason we admit kings and also the reason why they are not kings when they neglect religion. From these doctrines, I say, it is inferred by Carbone that "It is lawful to wish the death of a tyrant or of a favorer of heretics, even though he dies in mortal sin." To wish and to do so are naturally the same fault. Still, although it is "A sin to offer myself to martyrdom simply out of the weariness of life," according to Mazzolini, or according to Navarrus "To wish death simply out of impatience, anger, shame, poverty, or misfortune"—even to wish for heaven simply for my own happiness—nevertheless, Saint Paul certainly had some permissible reasons to desire to be released and to be with Christ.

Besides that, by his leave, we desire many things that are against the sense of nature. But to grant that we may wish death in order to be in heaven, although Peter Martyr, as noted above, is of the same persuasion, is a larger scope and somewhat more dangerous and slippery a grant than we are urging towards, because only the interest and good of the party seems to be considered. Nevertheless, Manoel de Sa extends it further: "We may wish someone's sickness for his correction. We may wish someone's death for the good of the state. We may even wish death to our enemy who is likely to do us much harm, or to avoid something particularly damaging to us. We may rejoice at our enemy's death, even for the consideration of our own deliverance." All of these hold as well if we are urged for similar reasons to wish our own death.

To conclude this point that it may be lawful to wish our own death, I shall just tell a story that, although it is only matter-of-fact, if it is that much, is of a person whose acts govern and persuade very many, as far as rules go. In the life of Philip Neri, who in our age instituted the last religious order approved and established in the Church of Rome, we read that he was entreated, as he commonly was in such desperate cases, to come to one Paulus Maximus, a youth of fourteen years, who was then ready to depart this life because of sickness. Before Neri could finish his sacrifice and the service had begun—even before the message reached him—the young man died. When he had been dead about half an hour, Neri came. After he had used some loud exclamations, the youth revived, looked up, and talked in secret with Neri for a quarter of an hour. When the discourse ended, Neri gave him his choice, whether he would live or die, and when the boy chose death he gave him permission to die again. This was the greatest miracle in that whole book—if anybody should believe all that are in it, for there are attributed to Neri stranger things than the Book of Conformities imagined about Saint Francis. (I believe the author, like Xenophon or Plato or Sir Thomas More, meant to imagine and idealize rather than to write a credible history, although Sedulius has defended the book lately and with much earnestness.) At any rate, this much is established: whether fable or history, the opinion of those who authored this book is that it was lawful for Maximus to wish his own death, since a man of so much sanctity as Neri approved, seconded, and accomplished his choice.

5. The next species of homicide in Toledo's division is homicide by permission. When it is done to ourselves, the scholastics usually called it desertion or dereliction and negative death.

I find no instance of this species to be more obnoxious or indefensible than the one that is so common with our delinquents; namely, to stand mute at the bar of justice. To be sure, civil laws, which often force us to choose the lesser of two evils (that is to say, the least hurtful to civility and society) and must sometimes allow a particular mischief rather than a general inconvenience, may excuse standing mute at the bar. By the law of conscience, no case may become so entangled and perplexed that one is forced to choose anything naturally evil, but no man has as yet, to my knowledge, impugned our custom of standing mute. Thus it strikes me that our church as well as our state justifies this desertion of ourselves for so low and worldly a consideration as saving our temporal estate or escaping the ignominy of another death.

To discern better how far these omissions, desertions, and exposings of ourselves are allowed us, I must first interpret a rule of Soto's: "That charity begins with itself is to be understood only in spiritual things." For I may not commit a sin, in the language of the scholastics, to save the goods, honor, or life of the pope, but for temporal things I must prefer others before myself if a public profit will recompense my private damage. I must also lay down another rule from Navarrus, "That as for myself, so for my neighbor whom I an bound to love as myself" I may expose goods to safeguard honor, I may expose honor for life, and I may expose life for spiritual profit. To these I must join a third rule from Maldonado, "That no man is at any time forced to exercise his privilege." Writes Ennenckel, "Every man is bound to know the written law, but privileges and exemptions from that law he excusably may be ignorant of, and in such ignorance transgress them." From this it is safely inferred that, because every man naturally has the privilege to resist force with force, he is thereby authorized to lay violent hands upon the pope's life (as Gerson exemplifies) or upon the emperor's (as Ennenckel exemplifies) when either of them exceeds the limits of his magistracy. For then the party becomes the deputy and lieutenant to nature, which is a sovereign common and equal to them all.

I may waive this benefit if I will, and I may suffer myself to be killed even by a thief rather than kill him in his mortal sin. Our countryman, Sayer, holds this as the common opinion from Soto, Navarrus, Cajetan, and many others. None that I have seen takes exception to it in any person other than a soldier or one who has the lives and dignities of others so wrapped up in their own that they cannot give themselves away except by betraying others. Such desertion seems to accord with natural reason, because it is found in all laws. Even in the Koran we read, "He who takes vengeance is not answerable for it, but he who patiently suffers a wrong acts best."

Our law punishes a man who kills another in his own necessary defense with the loss of goods, and it delivers him from death not by acquittal but by pardon. This seems to me to pronounce plainly that it is not lawful to defend my life by killing another, which is farther than any of the others went. When I compare our two laws—one that if I defend myself I am punished, and the other (aforementioned) that if I kill myself I am punished in the same manner and measure—they seem to me to be somewhat perplexed and captious.

Just as I may take leave of my natural privilege of defending myself, so may I obtain help from any extrinsic or accessory source that by chance or by providence (if God does not reveal his will) is presented to me. "For a man condemned to death is not bound in conscience to redeem his life with money, although by law of place he might do it," according to Sa. Saint Thomas Aquinas says that "He who is condemned to die kills himself if he does not seize an opportunity to escape by flight when it is presented, and likewise if he refuses meat when he is condemned to be starved," but the whole stream is against him—Soto, Navarro, Cajetan, and Sayer. Dr. Navarrus adds that in these days a man is bound to starve rather than to eat meat offered to idols, even though one now is not so likely to be a symbol of this idolatrous perversity.

Therefore, these authorities say that Aquinas's opinion that a man is bound to use his privilege to safeguard his life is only true when he does not waive it for some end better and worthier than our natural life. All spiritual advantages are of this sort. In these cases they all agree that we may abandon and forsake ourselves.

We may step farther yet into this kind of desertion, for we may offer ourselves for the good of our neighbor. The temporal life cannot be more precious than our soul, which, strictly speaking, is murdered by every sin consented unto. Yet Chrysostom says, "No praise is enough to give to Sarah for consenting to lie and to submit herself to adultery to save her husband's life."

I know that Saint Augustine is earnest against this point. But his earnestness turns on a matter of fact, for he denies that either Abraham or Sarah consented to any sin. When he disputes whether according to law Sarah by Abraham's consent might expose herself to save his life (Gen. 12:10–20, 20:1–18), he is also much troubled by the example of one who was prisoner under Acindynus, a prefect under Constantius, because of debt to the state. When his wife was solicited by a rich man who would give her enough to free her husband if he could possess her for one night, by her husband's consent she earned his liberty in that manner. In the end Augustine leaves it neutral for any man to think self-homicide either lawful or unlawful in such a necessity, although his own opinion indeed declines from it. Bonaventure denies that for the temporal good of another I may willingly offer my life, but he grounds it on the same reason that Augustine does, that we may not love another more than ourselves, which in this case we seem to be doing.

But many of the Fathers such as Jerome, Ambrose, and Lactantius, and many scholastics such as Aquinas, Francisco de Vitoria, Soto, Bañez, and infinite others are against him. They answer Saint Augustine that in this case a man does not prefer his friend over himself, but he prefers acts of virtue and of friendship, as things of a more spiritual nature, over his own temporal life.

That for the spiritual good of another a man should expose his own life is an unresisted doctrine. Sayer says, "It is under precept." Thus a curate is bound to baptize and to anoint in the time of a plague. Yes, it is an act of virtue, though not of necessity, as in the curate's case, "To visit a sick man in such a time, although you are a private man and your aim is not spiritual comfort," says Sa.

We may proceed even further, for we may lawfully dispossess ourselves of that which has been afforded us and without which we can have no hope of sustaining our lives. In a persecution, for example, a private man, having food sufficient only to sustain one man, may give it to a public person and so perish. Only Soto denies that in a shipwreck, after we have both been in equal danger, if I catch a fish and get myself something to sustain me, I may give this to my father or to a magistrate. Here Soto stands against the force of Navarrus, Toledo, Francisco de Vitoria, and many others.

The farthest and uttermost degree of this desertion is inordinate, indiscreet, voluntary fasting. As it is written into the canons, Saint Jerome says, "By such an immoderate innocence and indiscreet singing of psalms and offices a man loses his dignity and incurs the reputation of madness." About this writing Navarrus says that Saint Jerome pronounces "Indiscreet fasting that shortens the life" to be self-homicide "if the party perceives that it works that effect, even if it is done without any intention to shorten his life and done in order to be better able to satisfy God." Speaking of the same intention, he adds in another place, "It makes no difference whether you are long in killing yourself or do it at once."

Cassian expressly says, "That friar killed himself who, having vowed in his journey to eat nothing unless God himself gave him meat, refused to eat when thieves who customarily killed travelers at that place came and presented him bread." Although he says he killed himself, he nevertheless imputes to him nothing but indiscretion.

Therefore, Bosquier says, "Our savior Christ did not exceed forty days in his fast so he would not seem a self-homicide." He interprets the words, "He hungered," to mean, "Then he perceived his body to languish and suffer detriment by fasting." For, if he had not hungered until then, his fasting would have had no virtue, so that he gave in when he found the state of his body impaired by fasting, still pursuing and imitating the superstition of the philosophers who taught that "While we strengthen the body, we are being made more mortal," and that "By attenuation we are made like God." How much the writers in the Roman Church allow and obliquely exhort these inordinate fasts and other disciplines appears from what I cited above from Scribanius—indeed, wherever they have occasion to speak of this matter. On that topic more than any other do they so often inculcate, "It was the practice of the devil to appear to Saint Francis and cry out to him that no man who kills himself with such maceration could be saved," which Bonaventure relates in his life of Francis.

They teach that we ought to outdo whatever others have done. They say, "The monks in Prester John's dominions fast strictly for fifty days, standing all the while in water up to the chin." They find in the chronicles of Konrad of Lichtenau, abbot of Ursperg, the story of a maid who fasted two years and a half after she had received [in communion] the body of our blessed savior. They say a desert monk fasted twenty-two years without eating or drinking anything. They say no fast can be too severe that is undertaken to reduce our body to tameness. Indeed Sayer says, "Although that tameness is already perfectly accomplished, still a man is bound to the fasts that are enjoined." Aquinas says, "Fasting, even without charity, washes away sin."

By this rigor of fasting they seem sure that our savior stayed awake all those forty days (Matt. 4:2, Mark 1:13, Luke 4:2), because, says Bosquier, "He who takes bed takes breakfast." But since it is unlikely that Moses slept in his forty days of conversation with God (Exod. 24:18), it is also unlikely that Christ did any less than he. Saint Francis is extolled by them for observing three Lents every year—just what Saint Jerome so detested in the Montanists—and, although their aims were different, still this shows that to some aims these enormous witherings of our bodies are allowable. For that reason John the Baptist's austerity (Matt. 3:4) is so much dignified, and Saint Peter's feeding on lupines, and Saint Matthew's living without meat. The Emperor Justinian "In an extreme sickness during Lent would take nothing but herbs, salt, and water." According to the Carthusian rule, even though it appears that meat would save the patient's life, he may not eat it. According to the Apostolic Constitutions, which Torres extols so much that by them he refuses much of the Reformed Church's doctrine, "A man must fast to death rather than receive any meat from an excommunicated person." In another chapter, "In a case of extreme necessity if anything is accepted from such a person, it may be bestowed in full, so that their alms may be burned and consumed to ashes—but not meat with which to nourish ourselves."

To end this section on desertion: since we may waive our defense that the law gives by leaving our case to a jury; since nature allows us to repel force with force; since I may without fleeing (or eating when I have the means) turn myself over to an executioner or a famine; since I *may* offer my life, even for another's temporal good, which I *must* do for his spiritual good; since I may give another my board in a shipwreck and so drown; since I may hasten my arrival in heaven by consuming penances; since all that is the case, it is a wayward and ignoble stubbornness in argument to say I must not kill myself but I may let myself die. As to affirmations and denials, of omissions and commissions, of injunctions and prohibitory commands, always the one implies and enwraps the other. If the matter can be resolved and governed only by an outward *act* and always by that, then if I forbear to swim in a river and so perish, because there is no act, I shall not be guilty. But I shall be guilty if I discharge at myself a pistol that I did not know was loaded and intended no harm, because there is an *act*.

Mariana the Jesuit seems to be of this latter opinion, as we shall have occasion to note in the next member and species of homicide, which is abstinence.

6. Before we come to that topic, we must consider another species of homicide, which is mutilation or maiming—although it neither is nor naturally could be included in Toledo's division.

In civil courts self-maiming is not subject to the same penalty as self-homicide. But if it is accompanied by the same malignity it is in conscience the same sin, especially towards ourselves, because it violates the same reason, that nobody may encroach upon the body over which he has no dominion.

For that reason it is also unlawful for us to deliver ourselves into bondage—which I mention here because it arises from the same ground, and I am loath to accord it a particular section. Yet the holy Paulinus, a confessor and bishop of Nola, than whom I find no man celebrated with more fame of sanctity and integrity, in order to redeem a widow's son delivered himself as a slave to the Vandals and was exported from Italy to Africa—when as a bishop he was needed in his place, I think, for it happened only five years before his death.

To return to mutilation, it is clear from the canons that with reference to illegality it counts as much and goes as far to have maimed as to have killed. A council at London in 1075 passed a canon that forbids a clergyman to be present at a judgment of death or of mutilation. Among the Apostolic Canons is this one, "He who castrates himself cannot be a clergyman because he is a homicide of himself and an enemy to God's creature." In our law, "To castrate is to maim." In the next canon it is said, "A clergyman who castrates himself must be deposed because he is a self-homicide. For that fault a layman must be excommunicated for three years, because he betrays his own life." Castration was therefore counted equivalent to killing. Calvin counted it so heinous that he built his argument against divorce on this ground, "God made them one body, and in no case is it lawful for a man to tear his own body." But if castration is as lawful as divorces are lawful, certainly the peremptory sentence against it must admit of some modification!

There are, of course, examples of holy men who have maimed themselves to disable themselves from taking on the burden of priesthood. One was Saint Mark the Evangelist, who to that end cut off his thumb.

Also, since our savior said, "Many should castrate themselves for the kingdom of heaven" (Matt. 19:12), Athenagoras fifty [actually, 150] years after Christ says that many did it. Apart from these examples, nobody doubts what Sayer says, "That a man unjustly detained to a sure execution may cut off the limb by which he is tied, if he has no other way to escape; or, being surrounded by dogs, he may cut off a hand and cast it to them in order to distract them while he escapes."

7. The last species of homicide in Toledo's argument is this: the last act is an actual helping and concurrence to it. Every step and degree conducing purposely to that end is by judges of conscience justly called homicide. So Arduino, reckoning up all poisons that have a natural malignity and tendency to destroy man's body, does not exclude a flea, although it never kills, because it tries to do so and does all the damage it can. He is diligent in assigning preservatives and restoratives against the flea.

Upon the Amalekite who told David he helped Saul die when he found him too weak to stab himself, David pronounced a judgment of death, for, he says, "Your own mouth has confessed that you have killed the Lord's anointed" (II Sam. 1:16). Mariana the Jesuit, whom I have cited above, reckons this actual concurring in one's own death as heavy as the act itself—as it seems, even though the party does not know it. After he decided how a heretical king might be poisoned, he was diligent in this prescription, "The king must not be constrained to take the poison himself, but some other way administer it to him. Therefore, it should be prepared and conveyed in some way other than meat or drink, because otherwise, either willingly or ignorantly, the king would kill himself." Thus he provides that the king who must die under the sins of tyranny and heresy must still be defended from concurring in his own death, even ignorantly, as though this were a greater sin.

Since, on this reading, the hastening of our death by such an act is the same as complete self-homicide, let us consider how far unreproved custom, example, and law either allow it or command it. That it is allowable seems to me somewhat proved in that "Before any man accuses him, a malefactor may go and declare his fault to the judge," according to Soto.

Among Italian narratives, the one in Sansovino concerning England has many marks and impressions of malice. He tells of a custom, which he falsely says is observed here. "Men condemned to be hanged are always accompanied to their executions by all their kindred, who then hang on their feet to hasten their end. Also, when a patient is abandoned by the physicians, his nearest kinsman strangles him with a pillow." The author had this much ground, that ordinarily at executions men, out of charity as they think, do so, and women who despair of sick persons' recovery used to take their pillows from under them and so let them die sooner. Have they any more dominion over these bodies than the persons themselves? Or if a man were able to do these things to himself, might he not do so? Or might he not with a safe conscience put so many weights in his pockets as would accomplish the stretching? I speak only comparatively; might he not do it as well as they?

In my understanding, such an act either by an executioner or a bystander is in no way justifiable, for it is an injury both to the party, whom a sudden pardon might redeem, and to the judge, who has appointed a painful death to deter others from crime. The breaking of the legs of crucified men (John 19:32), which was done to hasten death, was not allowed except by petition. The law might be much defrauded if such violence might be used where the breaking of the halter delivered the prisoner from death, as it does in some places. Good opinions concur that one should always do without doubt whatever makes for easy, or escapes painful, passage out of this life. In such cases a man may do things more allowably by his own act than a stranger may. For the law of nature inclines and excuses him. Others are forbidden by many laws to hasten his death, because they are otherwise interested only as parts of the whole body of the state, and thus it concerns them that justice be executed. We see that this, like the case of withdrawing the pillows, is ordinarily done and counted a pious deed. The Athenian executions were always by the hand of the offender in judgments of death by poison.

In the law of purgation assigned by God to ease a man on whom the spirit of jealousy had fallen, the woman was to take the water of curses and bitterness, which would make her infamous and make her belly swell and her thighs rot (Num. 5:11–22). Those forms of purgation that were called common ones lasted long, even in the church, for there is nothing extant against them until Steven V in the year 885. Charlemagne, in whom the church acknowledged enough piety, introduced one form more severe than the rest, which was to walk on nine burning harrows.

When a bishop named Brito was extrajudicially calumnied by the people for having gotten his laundress with child, after his innocence had prevailed so far with God that the one-month-old child, being adjured in the name of Christ, exonerated him, Brito did not accept it but chose and performed a kind of purgation by carrying burning coals upon his head. Evidently in England both kinds of trial by ordeal, by water and by fire, lasted until King John's time. Although men were forced to go into the ordeal of boiling water, that was only for the meaner sort, but to carry the three-pound weight of red-hot iron, which was for the purgation of persons of better quality, was an act (as all the foregoing were) in which a man must of necessity do something actually against himself and be the executioner of his own judgment. As long as these forms of purgation—and the other, by battle—were legal, they were lawfully done.

In Saint Dorotheus, who everywhere professed a love of the obedience that he himself called indiscreet, you will read many praises given
to men who not only forsook themselves but actually furthered their
destruction—although not effectually, which makes no difference, if it is
in dangers that men usually do not escape. He praises one friar who,
being commanded by his abbot to return one night, when the waters
were risen that night committed himself to a raging torrent in such an
act of obedience.

Another was bidden by his abbot to go into the town where he suspected he would fall into some temptation by a certain spectacle. He
went, but with the protestation that he hoped he was in the protection
not of God but of the one who sent him. But the most natural story to
our present purpose is this. A hoary old man, seeing his servant mistake
poison for honey and put it into his broth, ate it nevertheless and without
chiding. When the servant perceived it and exclaimed, "Sir, I have killed
you," he answered, "It's all the same, for if God would have had me eat
honey he would have directed your hand to the honey." We have sufficient testimony to the holiness of Joseph of Arimathaea who, being sent
by the apostles to preach the gospel, among other persecutions was constrained to drink poison, which necessarily involved the act that we now
discuss. How much did Saint Andrew contribute to his own crucifixion?
How much did Saint Lawrence contribute to his own broiling when he
called to the tyrant, "This side is done; turn the other, and then eat"?
"Great men make precepts by their deeds," says Quintilian. These acts of
men who otherwise are counted holy may always be good warrants and
examples to us, when the cause is not prejudged by any greater authority
such as scripture or councils, nor that very act accused by any author.

But to stay no longer with examples, among casuists I observe that
the greater number denies that it is lawful for a condemned man to do
the last, immediate act that leads to his death, such as the drinking of
poison, but they agree that he may do the acts that are somewhat more
removed.

Francisco de Vitoria defines even this act of drinking poison as lawful.
Thus among them it is not clear whether or not a man may do it. Indeed, in
very many cases it is not only lawful to do as much without any
condemnation, but also it is necessary, and by their rules sinful, to omit it.
Curates must go into infected houses to administer the sacraments. If a
priest enters a woods where three wait to kill him, and one of them,
repenting of that purpose, meets him and under the seal of confession
discloses the fault, the priest is bound to go forward to a certain death in the
woods rather than by returning let the others know that he learned in
confession of their plan. So peremptory is their doctrine, whatever be their
practice, against revealing confessions. Although this may perhaps seem a
wanton case, framed on impossible happenings, as Soto counts it, the reason

may have this use: that although self-preservation is divine natural law and the seal of confession is only divine positive law, still, because the circumstances are not the same, in this case a public good must be preserved above his private life. Thus we may do some acts ourselves that probably—even certainly, as far as human knowledge goes—lead to our destruction, which is the nearest step to the last act of doing it entirely ourselves.

8. We spoke of this last act of self-homicide while considering the law of nature and must speak of it again when we come to understand those texts in scripture that seem to aim towards it. Before we conclude this part about the law of reason, we may aptly present such deductions, comparisons, and consequences as may reasonably seem to annihilate or diminish this fault. Because most will be grounded either in the conscience of the doer or in the church's opinion of the deed when it is done, we will consider how far an erring conscience may justify any act. Then we will produce some examples of persons guilty of this who were nevertheless canonized by the church's admitting them into the martyrology and assigning them their feasts, offices, vigils, and such religious celebrations. We need make no use of the example of Pythagoras, who rather than offend his philosophical conscience either by treading on the beans himself or by suffering his scholars to speak before their time, delivered up himself and forty of his scholars to his enemy's sword.

To avoid the deceitful ambiguities and multiform entanglings of the scholastics, we will follow what is delivered for the common opinion. A conscience that errs justly, probably, and in good faith—that is, after all moral industry and diligence have been used (I do not mean exquisite diligence but such as is proportionate to the person and his quality and to the knowledge that that man is bound to have of that thing at that time)—is bound to act according to the misinformation and the mispersuasion thus contracted. Moreover, with a conscience that errs negligently or otherwise viciously and in bad faith, as long as the error remains and resides in the conscience, a man is bound *not* to act against his conscience. In the first case, if one thinks in his conscience that he ought to lie to save an innocent person or that he ought to steal to save a famished man, he is a homicide if he does not lie or steal. In the second case, although he is not bound to any act, it is lawful for him to admit anything otherwise necessary.

This obligation that our conscience lays upon us is of stronger hold and of narrower band than the precept of any superior, whether a law or a person, and is so much of natural right that it cannot be infringed or altered by the benefit of divine indulgence, to use their own words. As that doctrine is to be gathered everywhere among the casuists, so it is well collected, amassed, argued, and confirmed, especially by Azorius.

If a man, after convenient and requisite diligence, despoiled of all human affection and self-interest and "Burning with the holy fire of good impatience," as Paulinus says, in conscience believes that he is invited by the spirit of God to do what Jonah, Abraham, and perhaps Samson did, who according to these rules can condemn this to be sin?

Thus I suspect there was some haste and precipitousness in the judgment of Cassian, otherwise a just esteemer and valuer of works of devotion and obedience, who pronounces the apparition of an angel to Heron the desert monk, who after fifty years was so intense and earnest in attending God's service and in religious negligence of himself that he would hardly omit Easter Day from his strict fasting, and being now full of the awareness of victories (so the panegyric says)—Cassian calls the apparition an illusion of the devil to make Heron destroy himself. Yet Heron, being drawn out of the well into which he had cast himself and living three days afterwards, persisted in a devout acknowledgment that it was the spirit of God that solicited him to do it. Heron died in such constant assurance and alacrity that Paphnutius the abbot, although at first in some suspense, did not number him among the self-homicides, who were persons reputed to have viciously killed themselves.

Nor may it necessarily be concluded that this act was therefore evil if it appeared to be from the devil. For Wier tells us of a maid whom the devil persuaded to go on a certain pilgrimage and at a certain altar to hear a mass for the recovery of her health. Surely if, as Vázquez holds, "It is not idolatry to worship the devil in an apparition if I think it is God," it can be no offense to believe him, after I have used all means to discern and distinguish! Those rules that are delivered ordinarily by which to know the devil are apparently false—a difference in his hands or feet, or some notable deformity of horns or a tail, of which Binsfeld seems confident of the first and Menghi of the second.

Even the rule that God always infuses or commands good things, if it is understood to apply to what is good in the common and natural course of events, is not always safe, for it did not hold in Abraham's case nor in that of the Israelites. Vázquez's first excuse, that such worship is not idolatry because by reason of our immediate relation to God we never arrest nor stop the devil by the way, will do no good in our case of believing. But his other excuse will help which he has in the same place; namely, that there may be an invincible ignorance, and that in such ignorance any exterior act whatever that proceeds from a sincere and pure intention of the mind is an act of true religion. More safely than the panegyric could say to Constantine, "His own wisdom is his deity," may we say of every man's conscience that is thus rectified.

Therefore, if they will still turn in their circle and say, God concurs in no evil, we say nothing is so evil but that it becomes good if God commands it. Moreover, self-homicide is not so naturally evil that it requires a special commission from God. Just as it becomes good if he commands it, so it becomes neutral if he removes the reasons conditioning the precept against it.

If they return to Saint Augustine's two reasons against Donatus—the first was, "We have authority to save your body against your will," and the second was, "None of the faithful ever did this act"—we are thereby hastened to the other consideration, how those who have done it have been esteemed by the Catholic Church.

A little needs to be said in passing about Saint Augustine's second reason. The first has very little force since, although it may be lawful to preserve a man who is willing to die, it is not always meritorious or obligatory to do so. Thus Ignatius so earnestly exhorted the Romans not to try to preserve him. Also, the civic crown, which was given to any who had rescued a citizen in the wars, was not given, even if he produced witnesses of the deed, unless the person so rescued confessed that he benefited thereby. In the second reason, why does Saint Augustine refer Donatus to examples? For if Donatus had produced any (as from credible and authentic stories he might have produced very many, and out of the scriptures that in Saint Augustine's opinion were canonical he might have alleged the examples of Eleazar and Razis), Saint Augustine was always provided with the refuge that it was special inspiration and not to be followed or imitated.

Had it been a good argument in Rome for 500 years that divorce was not lawful, because there was no example of it?—or for almost 2,000 years that a woman might not sue for divorce against her husband, because before Herod's daughter there was no example of it? But when the church has persevered so long not only in justifying but also in solemnizing many examples of self-homicide, are not Saint Augustine's disciples guilty of the same pertinacity that is imputed to Aristotle's followers who, defending the heavens to be unalterable because in so many ages nothing had been observed to have been altered, his scholars still stubbornly maintain his proposition, although by many experiences of new stars (according to Kepler) the reason that moved Aristotle now seems to be utterly defeated?

Having spoken this much about Saint Augustine and having purposely postponed the examples recorded in the scriptures for our third part, we will consider some examples registered in ecclesiastical history.

The church—whose dignity and constancy it well becomes that the rule of its own law always be justly said of itself, "What once was acceptable cannot later be unacceptable," unless new reasons interpose—celebrates on February 9 the birth (that is, the death) of the virgin and martyr Apollonia. After the persecutors had beaten out her teeth and vexed her with many other tortures, she was led to the fire. Being inflamed with a more burning fire of the Holy Ghost, she broke from the officer's grasp and leaped into the fire. For this act of hers many advocates take up her case and say that either the story is not certain (although the sources are Bede, Usuard, Ado, and, as Baronius says, others of the Latins), or else, says Sayer, you must answer that she was brought very near the fire and as good as thrown in, or else that she was provoked to do it by divine inspiration. Unless it was another divine inspiration—true charity—that moved the beholders back then to believe and the church ever since to acknowledge that she thus did a noble and Christian act to the special glory of God, this act of hers as well as of any others might have been calumnied to have been done out of weariness of life, or fear of relapsing, or haste to reach heaven, or the ambition of martyrdom.

The memory of Pelagia as a virgin and martyr is celebrated on June 9. To be sure, the history of this woman suffers some perplexity and gives occasion to doubt its truth. Ambrose says that she and her mother drowned themselves, and Chrysostom says that they flung themselves down from a house-top. And Baronius finds this knot so hard to disentangle that he says, "There is nothing we say to this." Nevertheless, the church, as I said, celebrates her act as though it were glad to take any occasion of approving such courage in such a cause, which was only preservation of chastity. "Their martyrdom," says Saint Augustine, "was always in the Catholic Church frequented by the utmost veneration."

Saint Ambrose, when his sister Marcellina consulted him directly on what might be thought of those who kill themselves in such cases (and it is agreed by all that the opinions of the Fathers are to be especially valued when they speak of a matter not incidentally or casually but directly and deliberately), answered, "We have an example of such a martyrdom in Pelagia." Then he presented to his sister this religious meditation, "Let us die if we may have leave or if we are denied leave, yet let us die. God cannot be offended with this when we use it only for a remedy and our faith takes away all offense. Here is no difficulty, for who is willing to die and cannot, since there are so many ways to death? I will not trust my hand lest it fail to strike home nor my breast lest it withdraw itself. I will leave no escape to my flesh, for we can die with our own weapons and without the benefit of an executioner." [Donne's paraphrase of Ambrose's account of Pelagia is continued in quotation marks.] "Then, having dressed herself as a bride and going into the water, she says, 'Here let us be baptized. This is the baptism where sins are forgiven and where a kingdom is purchased, and this is a baptism after which none sins. This water regenerates, this makes us virgins, this opens heavens, defends the feeble, delivers from death, and makes us martyrs. Only we pray to God that this water not scatter us but reserve us to one funeral.' Then they entered as in a dance, hand in hand, where the torrent was deepest and most violent. Thus they died, as their mother upon the bank called them 'These prelates of virginity, captains of chastity, and companions in martyrdom.'"

Before Ambrose we find that Eusebius was of the same persuasion.

He has the mother encouraging them by saying, "'You know how I have brought you up in the fear of God; and shall your nakedness, which the public air has not had permission to see, now be prostituted in the pools? Do not have so little faith in God that you fear death. Do not despise chastity so much that you live with shame, but with a pure and chaste death condemn this world.' And so, deluding their keepers as though they withdrew for natural necessities, they drowned themselves."

All authors of that time are so profuse in their praise of this deed that it is just to say of it what Pliny says of Nerva's adopting Trajan: "It was impossible that it should have pleased all when it was done, unless it had pleased all before it was done." For no author that I have lighted upon diminished the glory of these and others like them until Saint Augustine, out of his most zealous and fearful tenderness of conscience, began to seek out some ways how these self-homicides might be justified, because he suspected that this act was naturally exempt from blame. Even so, he always brings himself to such perplexity that either he must defend it and call into question the authority of a general consonance of all times and authors, or else retreat to that poor and improbable defense that it was done by divine inspiration. That can hardly be admitted in this case, where it was not their religion but only their chastity that was solicited and attacked. Nor can Saint Ambrose or Eusebius be brought to that opinion of special divine inspiration, because, speaking sincerely, even if in the mother's person, they incite them to it with reasons drawn from moral virtues.

Still, Saint Augustine's example, as it prevails very much and very justly for the most part, has drawn many others since him to the same interpretation of the same acts. When the kingdom of Naples came to be divided between Ferdinand V and Louis XII, the French army being admitted into Capua on the condition that it do no violence, among many outrages a virgin, unable to escape the fury of a licentious soldier, offered as a ransom to lead him to treasure, and so took advantage of a place in the wall to fling herself into the river. "This act," says Pedraza, "we must believe to be done by divine inspiration, because God loves chastity now as well as he ever did." Every side may find this escape easy if, being pressed with reasons, they may say as Peter Martyr does of the Egyptian midwives (Exod. 1:15–20) and Rahab (Joshua 2:1–7) and others, "If they lied, they did it on an impulse from God."

But as our custom has been, let us leave examples for rules—even though a concurrence of examples and either an express or interpretive approbation of them (much more a dignifying of them such as this) by the whole church and Catholic authors approved by that church is equivalent to a rule. To ease the reader and to continue my first resolution of not descending into many particulars, I will present only one rule. But it is so pregnant that from it may be derived many by which not only a man may but must do the whole and entire act of killing himself—which is to preserve the seal of confession. For although the rule in general is, "If a spider fall into the chalice, the wine may be changed, because nothing abominable ought to be taken on the occasion of this sacrament," so it may be, if the priest after consecration comes into the knowledge that the wine is poisoned, "lest the chalice of life be turned into death." But if he knows this by confession from his assistant or anybody else and cannot by any diversion or disguise keep from disclosing that this was confessed to him except by drinking it, even if it is poison he must drink it.

Because men of more abundant reading, active discourse, and conclusive judgment will easily provide themselves with more reasons and examples to this purpose, it will satisfy me to have awakened them this much and shown them a mark to direct their meditations upon. So I may proceed to the third part, which is the law of God.

THE THIRD PART: OF THE LAW OF GOD

Distinction I

1. The light that issues from the moon best represents and expresses what we call in ourselves the light of nature. As that in the moon is permanent and always there, and yet unequal, various, pale, and languishing, so is our light of nature changeable. At the outset shining at full light, it soon waned and, through our departing farther and farther from God, declined on account of general sin to almost a total eclipse. God, later coming nearer to us first through the law and then through grace, enlightened and repaired it again, conveniently to his ends, for the further exercise of his mercy and justice. Then there are those artificial lights that we ourselves make for our use and service here, such as fires, tapers, and so forth. They resemble the light of reason, as we interpreted that term in our second part.

Although the light of these fires and tapers is not as natural as the moon's, still, because they are more domestic and obedient to us, we distinguish particular objects better by them than by the moon. So by the arguments, deductions, and conclusions that we ourselves beget and produce, being more serviceable and subordinate because they are our creatures, particular cases are made more clear and evident to us. With these we can be bold, put them to any use, examine and prove their truth or likelihood, and make them answer as long as we ask. But the light of nature, with a solemn and arrogant majesty, will speak only once and neither give a reason nor endure examination. Of these two kinds of light the first is too weak and the other false, for color is only the object of sight, and we do not trust candlelight to discern colors.

We therefore have the sun, the fountain and treasure of all created light, for an emblem of that third kind and best light of our understanding, which is the word of God. "The commandment is a lamp and the law a light" (Prov. 6:23), says Solomon. But since weak, credulous men sometimes think they see two or three suns when they see nothing but meteors or other appearances, so many men are transported with similar facility or dazzling. For some of their opinions they think they have the light and authority of scripture, when (God knows) truth, the light of divine scriptures, against their viewpoint, is removed to the farthest possible distance.

They take any small text of scripture that mistakenly appears to them to be of use in justifying any opinion of theirs. Then, since the word of God has that precious nature of gold so that a little quantity by reason of faithful tenacity and malleability can be made to cover 10,000 times as much as any other metal, they extend that small text so far, and labor and beat it to such a thinness that it is hardly any longer the word of God. They do so simply to give their reasons a little tincture and color of gold, even though they have lost all its weight and value.

But since the scripture itself teaches that "No prophecy in the scripture is of private interpretation" (II Peter 1:20), the whole church is not bound and enclosed by the fancy of any one (or of a few) who, being content to put themselves to sleep with any opinion and lazy prejudice, dream up arguments to establish and authorize it.

A professed interpreter of dreams, Artemidorus, tells us that "No dream of a private man may be interpreted to signify public business." This I say, because of all the texts in scripture that are alleged for the doctrine that we now examine hardly one, except the precept, "You shall not kill" (Exod. 20:13), is offered by any two authors. Rather, to one one text, and to another another text, seems directly to govern in the point. To me, to allow truth her natural and comely boldness, *no* texts govern except those that seem to look towards self-homicide.

In going over all the sentences that I have gathered from many authors and in presenting helpful answers to and interpretations of them, I shall forbear the names of the authors who produced them so impertinently, lest I seem to reveal their nakedness or even to accuse them of prevarication. If any divine thinks the cause or persons are injured herein and counts me worthy of being led back to the other opinion, with the same charity that provoked me and that (I thank God) has accompanied me from the beginning, I beseech him to take so much advantage from me and my instruction that he will do it without bitterness. He will better see the way, better show it, and better sail through it if he raises no storms.

May such men also, since they are "Fishers of men" (Matt. 4:19), hunt us into their nets for our own good. But perhaps there is some mystical interpretation belonging to the canon that allows clergymen to hunt. They may do it by nets and snares but not by dogs, for clamor and bitings are forbidden them. I have been sorry to see that even Beza himself, writing against an adversary and a cause equally and extremely obnoxious, simply by allowing his zeal too much fuel raged against the man and, neglecting or only forbidding the cause, has given answer to Ochino's book on polygamy with less thoroughness and satisfaction than either becomes his learning and watchfulness or befits his use and custom.

Distinction II

1. In all the judicial and the ceremonial law put forth by Moses, who was more particular in his laws than any others, there is no abomination, indeed no mention, of self-homicide. He teaches what we shall and shall not eat, wear, and speak, yet he says nothing against this.

2. The first text that I find offered against us is Genesis 9:5–6, "I will require your lifeblood; at the hand of every beast I will require it and at the hand of man; even at the hand of a man's brother will I require the life of man; whoever sheds a man's blood, by man shall his blood be shed."

Lavater, a very learned man of the Reformed Church, says that the Jews understand this text to imply self-homicide. But shall we put ourselves under the Jews' yoke, asks Buxtorf, so that "If we find in the rabbis things contrary to nature we must dare to accuse nothing but our own weakness, because their word is God's word, and if they contradict one another, still both are from God"? Nicholas of Lyra, who seldom departs from the Jews in matters not controverted between them and us, mentions no such exposition, yet he expounds the text in more than one way and with enough liberty and straying afar. Manoel de Sa, who in his notes is more curious and superstitious in restoring all the Hebraisms and oftentimes their interpretations than perhaps the Jews would desire at his hands, offers no other sense than what the words present. Nor can self-homicide fall within the threat and punishment of that law, for how can the magistrate shed the blood of one who has killed himself?

3. The next is Deuteronomy 32:39, "I kill, and I give life," from which it is concluded that all authority over life and death is from God and none is in ourselves. But shall we dare to condemn utterly all those states and governments in which fathers, husbands, and masters had jurisdiction over children's, wives', and servants' lives? If we dare, how shall we defend any magistracy, if this text is so strictly interpreted? Or, if it admits exceptions, why may not our case be included among them?

However, that this text is incongruously brought to bear on the topic appears from the words that follow it, "There is none that can deliver out of my hand." Moreover, since this is a verse of the divine poem that God himself made and delivered to Moses as a stronger and more slippery insinuation and impression into the Israelites' hearts than the language of any law would make, it only expresses that the mercies and judgments of God are safe and removed from any human hindrance or interruption. Similarly, in another song of thanks made by Samuel's mother the same words are repeated, "The lord kills and makes alive" (I Sam. 2:6); this is because God had given her a son when she was past hoping for one. That text also in Tobit 13:12 is fitly paralleled with this one, "He leads to hell and brings up, nor is there any who can avoid his hand" (Tobit 13:2). Can these two texts be twisted from their purpose to mean that none but God may have jurisdiction over our temporal life? Also, the text from Wisdom 16:13 that is always joined to this issue signifies the same as these, "For you have the power of life and death," which is spoken of his miraculous curing by the brazen serpent. All four of these texts have one concern and aim, and none of them looks toward our question.

4. In the order of the divine books, the next text produced is Job 7:1, "The life of man upon earth is military service." Although our translation makes it out to say, "Is there not a time appointed to man upon earth?" the Latin text is cited to this purpose by some who are not addicted to the Vulgate edition, because in Latin it seems better to afford an argument against self-homicide. From it they infer that we may not depart at our own pleasure from the battle. But because only the metaphor and neither the extending of it nor the inference from it is taken from the scripture, it carries with it no strong obligation.

Nor does it deserve much earnestness by way of answer. Still, to follow up the allusion a bit, "A soldier may by law be ignorant of the law and is not much accusable if he transgresses it." According to another law, if "A soldier whose presence is necessary for the security of the army is absent by virtue of a public cause, his absence shall be interpreted to be so." Even toward those who killed themselves in the army the laws were not severe, as we noted in the second part, if they had any color of just cause. Therefore, this figurative argument profits nothing, especially since it is taken from the text where the intent of Job was to prove that our felicity and the end toward which our actions are bent is not in this life. Rather, just as wars work toward peace so we labor here toward death, toward the happiness we shall have hereafter. Thus, whoever was the author of the letter to Abgar bearing Christ's name does not make Christ say that when he has done that for which he was sent here he will come to Abgar and take his offer of half his kingdom, but that when he has done his work he will return to him who sent him; that is, he will die. Therefore, if either side of the issue has advantage from this text of Job, we have it.

5. Much more does our side have advantage from the other text from Job 7:15, "Therefore my soul chooses rather to be strangled and to die than to be in my bones." From this they infer that if it had been lawful to die, Job would have done it. Apart from the wretched poverty and feebleness of this kind of negative argument, since Job did not do it he was not allowed to do it, we may perceive from the whole frame of the story that God had chosen him for another use, as an example of extreme patience. Whatever appears in Job's case, he might not lawfully do it because he could intend nothing but his own ease. Still Job, whose sanctity I think it a sacrilege to diminish (whether he was a real or a

fictional person), by their confession strayed so far towards killing himself as to wish his death and to curse his birth, for the whole third chapter is a bitter and malignant invective against his life and a violent wishing for his own death.

Sextus Senensis gives so literal an answer that it makes no sense, "In cursing his birthday, which then was past, he cursed nothing." Saint Gregory the Great gives so mystical an answer that it makes no sense, "There is a second birth into sin in this world, and Job cursed his entrance into that birth." Since these words might readily be taken for an inordinate wishing for death, Gregory provides them also with a mystical interpretation. For the Latin reading, *suspendium eligit anima mea* (my soul chooses hanging), he says, "This was a spiritual hanging, which was only an elevation of the mind, as Saint Paul said, 'With Christ I have been crucified on the cross'" (Gal. 2:20).

Beyond the fact that this escape will not do when the original words are considered, the very next verse is, "I loathe my life; fruitlessly do I live on" (Job 7:16). In the twentieth verse [actually, Job 7:19] he chides God by the name of "O, you preserver of men" as being angry that he preserved him, "Being now a burden to himself, and would not leave him alone while he might swallow his spittle." He ends the chapter thus, "If you seek for me in the morning, I shall not be found" (Job 7:21). I say this only to show that one whom nobody has exceeded in holiness may, without any twisting of his words, be argued to have stepped far toward a purpose of killing himself. Whoever wishes to give any other construction to his words will not displease me, but he will not impair the strength of our proposition.

I confess that I have not read anybody who expounds these words of Job this directly, and I know that the general opinion about his despairing held by the Anabaptists is much discredited. Apart from all that, it is neither just nor ingenuous to condemn everything that a condemned man says, for even a leprous man may have one clean hand with which to give and take. Saint Jerome is inexcusable for his slippery zeal in his behavior toward Vigilantius. The Council of Trent itself is obnoxious for condemning the names of authors instead of their books. Moreover, the Anabaptists differ from me in their aim and purpose, for they impute despair to Job only to discredit the authority of the book, which they schismatically labor to tear from the canon of scripture. With the consent of all Christian churches admitting the book to the canon, I justly say that Job might keep his sanctity and the book its dignity, and still he might have intended to kill himself. Very many reverend authors in the Reformed Church who are not rashly to be dismissed have imputed to our most blessed savior as near approaches to a more dangerous kind of despair than we impute to Job, without putting down him or his scriptures.

6. I find also another text, Job 2:4, thrust forth, "Skin for skin, and all

that ever a man has he will give for life." From these words they argue a natural love in us for this life.

Let it be true (although the devil says it, for the words are his) that our sensitive nature is too indulgent towards this life. I fear I have offended and surfeited you in the first part with examples of merely natural and sensitive men who have chosen death. Still, will that prove that our reasonable nature may in no case correct the enormity? This is as strong against God's outwardly calling us to him by sickness or persecution as it is against any such inward motions.

7. As improperly and unprofitably to their ends and purpose they offer the text from Ecclesiasticus 30:16, "There is no wealth above the wealth of physical health." I place it here, although out of order, because of the affinity between this text and the last one, and since one answer is at least enough for both. While this text may prove that we naturally love this body—the text is not about the safety of the body, as if all men desired that the body might live, but about bodily health while it does live—still it does not prove that we may in no case abandon it.

8. The most proper and direct and the strongest text, for it is of moral law, is the commandment, "You shall not kill" (Exod. 20:13). This text is cited by all to this purpose.

I must be allowed to depart here from the opinion of Saint Augustine, who thinks that this commandment is more earnestly bent upon a man's own self than upon another, because here there is no addition, as there is in the other, "Against your neighbor" (Exod. 20:16). Certainly I am as much forbidden by the commandment falsely to accuse myself as my neighbor, although he alone is named in it. By this one I am as much forbidden to kill my neighbor as myself, although nobody is named. What holds within the compass of the commandment may also hold within the exceptions to it. Although the words are general, "You shall not kill," we may kill beasts. Magistrates may kill men. A private man in a just war may not only kill, contrary to the sound of this commandment, but he may kill his father, contrary to another one!

When two natural laws contrary to one another occur, we are bound to the one that is of the stricter bind. All laws concerning the honor of God and faith also concern, by virtue of charity, the Second Table of commandments, which is directed toward our neighbor. If, therefore, there could be a necessity that I must do an act of idolatry or kill, I would be bound by the latter commandment and commit idolatry.

If perchance a public, exemplary person, who had a just assurance that his example would govern the people, should be forced by a tyrant to do an act of idolatry (even if under the circumstance he could satisfy his own conscience that he did not sin in doing it) and so scandalize and endanger the people, if the matter were so carried out and disguised that in no way he could let them know that he did it under constraint and not voluntarily, I say by this rule that perhaps he had better kill himself.

A safe rule of Ennenckel's is, "It is not possible to modify divine law unless the modification itself agrees with divine law." But since it is not thought by Navarrus a violation of that rule, "To kill by public authority, or in a just war, or in defense of one's life or of another's," why may not our case be as safe and innocent? If anyone importunes me to show the privilege or exemption of this case from the commandment, I may with Soto hurl it back and call for their privilege to kill a day-thief or any man in defense of another.

As these laws may be logically deduced from the conformity of other laws and from a general authority that God has afforded to all sovereigns to provide as necessities arise, so may our case be derived as well from the necessary obligation that always lies upon us of preferring God's glory over all human concerns. We cannot be put upon to show or to plead any exemption unless, when such a case arises, we say that the case never was within reach of that law. The same is true of all the other things that we heretofore called exemptions. Whatever might have been done prior to the law (as this might, if it is against neither nature nor justice, from both of which we claim to have acquitted it), this commandment never fell upon that or extended to it.

9. I have also found a text urged from Wisdom 1:12, "Seek not death in the error of your life." It is always coupled with a text from Deuteronomy 4:24, so that by collating the two it appears that what is forbidden there is idolatry and by death is meant the second death of eternal damnation, or the way to it.

So this distinction, which was intended for the texts cited from the books of the Old Testament, shall here end, and to the next we assign those of the New Testament.

Distinction III

1. The first that I have observed in the New Testament is Matthew 4:6, where the devil tempts Christ, "If you are the son of God, cast yourself down." With all expositors I confess that this was a temptation to vainglory and therefore applies to our case. We claim that we work somewhat to the service of God and the advancement of his glory when we allow self-homicide to be done. It is a very slippery passage, and a devout man by the nature of devotion would be more likely to err that way than a worldly man, except that the hand of God is extended to protect such men.

Taken directly, this text will not shake or defy our proposition, for although Christ would neither satisfy the devil nor disclose who he was, when it served his own purposes he did as much as the devil tempted him to do in this text or the other, both in changing the species and nature of water into wine and in exposing himself to certain danger when he walked upon the waters. Christ neither rejected difficulties nor abstained from miracles when he knew he profited the beholders. I do not say that in any other case than when we are probably and excusably assured that it is to a good end may self-homicide be lawful for us.

2. The next text is in the Acts of the Apostles 16:28, "The keeper of the prison drew out his sword and would have killed himself, supposing the prisoners to be gone, but Paul cried, 'Do yourself no harm, for we are all here.'" To this I say that by the same spirit by which Paul, being in the inner prison in the dark, knew what the keeper thought and what he was about to do, he also knew God's purpose to be glorified in the conversion of the keeper and his family. Therefore, he not only restrained the keeper from his intent, which was inordinate and for his own sake, to escape punishment (in which we still may observe how readily man's nature inclines him to this remedy), Paul also forbore to take benefit from the miracle by escaping. Although he rescues the keeper, he betrays himself.

Thus Calvin poses to himself this objection to the text, that "Paul, seeing all hope of escape to consist in the death of the keeper, neglected the means of liberty that God offered him, when he restrained the keeper from killing himself"; Calvin answers only that "He had a knowledge and insight into God's purpose and decree." Otherwise, if he had not had that understanding (which very few achieve), it seems he ought to have let the keeper proceed, in order to facilitate his means of escaping.

3. This also infers an answer to another text of Saint Paul, where he rids and discharges himself and his fellow apostles of having taught this doctrine, "That a man might do evil in order that good might come of it" (Rom. 3:8). Consequently it is well and by just inference pronounced that he forbids that doctrine. We also humbly subscribe to the same rule and interpret it just as Saint Paul intended it, of things made evil by nature and not by circumstance. We agree in these things also, when any such circumstance does make them evil, if another contrary circumstance does not preponderate and overrule this one. We take liberty to illumine this point with a larger discourse.

God always makes others his executioners of the evils that seem to us to be evils of punishment, of which death is. The greatest of all these, hardness of heart, although it is spiritual, is not worked immediately by God himself, as his spiritual comforts are, but occasionally and by desertion. In these cases God sometimes employs his angels, sometimes the magistrate, and sometimes ourselves. Still, all that God does in this life in any of these cases is only medicine, for even the blinding and hardening of the heart are sent to further salvation in some and are inflicted medicinally.

These ministers and instruments of his are our physicians, and we may not refuse any bitterness, not even that which is naturally poison, since we are wholesomely corrected by them. As in the case of cramps, which are contortions of the sinews, or of rigors and stiffness in the muscles, we may bring about in ourselves a fever to thaw them, or we may bring about a burning fever to recondense and retemper our blood, so in all rebellions and disobediences of our flesh we may minister to ourselves such corrections and remedies as the magistrate might, if the deed was perfectly plain. Even though for the prevention beforehand of evil we may perform all the offices of a magistrate upon ourselves, in such secret cases it is debatable whether or not we have the authority to do so afterwards, especially in capital matters. Since at this time we need not affirm precisely that authority, I shall not now examine further the extent of that power.

Rather, I go on to the kind of evil that must necessarily be understood in this text of Paul's, which is what we count as naturally evil. Even in that, the bishops of Rome have exercised their power to give dispensation for bigamy, which according to their doctrine is directly against God's commandment and therefore naturally evil. Nicholas V dispensed a bishop in Germany to consult with witches for the recovery of his health. It would be easy to amass many cases of similar presumption. In like manner the imperial law tolerates usury, prescribing in bad faith, and deceit of the public, and it expressly allows witchcraft—to good purposes. "Conformably to which law," Paracelsus says, "it is all one whether God or the devil cures, just so the patient gets well."

Thus the canons have prescribed certain rules for doing evil—when we are overtaken with perplexities, to choose the least serious case. Saint Gregory gives a natural example: "A man confronting a high wall and forced to leap it would choose the lowest part of the wall." Agreeing with all these, the casuists say that "In extreme necessity I do not sin if I induce a man to lend me money usuriously. The reason is that I incline him to a lesser sin, usury, when otherwise he would be a homicide by virtue of not relieving me."

God himself is said to work evil in us after this fashion, because when our heart is full of evil purposes he governs and disposes us to this evil rather than to that one. In this case, although the virtue and the evil are ours, still the order is from God, and it is good. Indeed, he positively inclines one to some certain evil in that he infuses into a man some good thoughts by which he, out of his viciousness, takes occasion to think he is better off to do some other sin than the one he intended to do. Since all these laws and practices agree that we sometimes do such evil not only for express and positive good but to avoid greater evil, it all seems to me to be against that doctrine of Saint Paul's.

Whatever any human power may dispense us from we may dispense ourselves from in extreme necessity, in the impossibility of recourse to better counsel, in the case of an erring conscience, and in many such cases, since the canon about two evils leaves it to our natural reason to judge, value, compare, and distinguish which of the two evils will occur. Since, for all of this, it is certain that no such dispensation, either from another or from myself, so alters the nature of the thing that it becomes thereby more or less evil, there appears to me no other safe interpretation but this one, that there is no external act that is naturally evil, and that circumstances condition such acts and give them their nature. In this way scandal can make heinous at a given time something that is not heinous if some person goes out of the room or winks.

The law itself is given us as a light that we might not stumble. We need it, but not to see what is naturally evil, for such evil we see naturally, and it was so even before the law declared it to us. Rather, we need this light to see what would be evil (that is, produce evil effects) if we did it at a certain time and under such and such circumstances.

That law is not itself absolutely good but good to the extent and in such respects that what it forbids is evil. Pico, comparing the law to the firmament (as Moses meant the word) observes that on the second day, when God made the firmament (Gen. 1:6), he did not say that it was good, as he did of every other day's work, but it was not evil; for then, says Pico, it could not have received the sun, for if it had been good it would not have needed it. He reprehends the Manichaeans for saying that the law was evil, while he holds to the text of Ezekiel 20:25 that it was not good.

The evil, therefore, that is forbidden by Saint Paul in this text is either acts of infidelity that no dispensation can deliver from the reach of the law or else acts that by our nature and reason and by the approbation of nations are counted evil or are declared by law or custom to be evil. Because of their ordinary evil effects, these cast guiltiness upon the doer ordinarily and for the most part, and always unless his case is exempt and privileged. This consideration moved Chrysostom, whom I cited before, to think a lie and a consent to adultery were not evil in Sarah. The same consideration corrected Saint Augustine's squeamishness so far that he leaves us free to think what we will of that wife's act who to pay her husband's debt sold herself for one night.

If any of these things had once been naturally evil, they could never recover from that sickness. As I intimated before, those things that we call miracles were written in the story of God's purpose as precisely (and were as sure to come to pass as the sun's rising and setting) and as naturally in nature's whole compass, for in *that* book of God nothing is written between the lines. In his eternal register, where he foresees all our acts, he has preserved and defended neutral things from ordinary corruption—of evil purpose, of inexcusable ignorance, of scandal, and similar neutral corruptions. So he is said to have preserved our blessed Virgin from original sin in her conception.

To those who do not studiously distinguish circumstances or do not see the doer's conscience and the testimony of God's spirit, some of those acts of ours may at first taste have some of the brackishness of sin. So it was with Moses' killing of the Egyptians (Exod. 12:12), for which there appears no special calling from God. Because this does not happen often, Saint Paul would not embolden us to do any of those things that are customarily reputed to be evil.

If others are delighted with the more ordinary interpretation of this text, that it speaks of everything we call sin, I will not reject that interpretation, provided they do not make the apostle's rule (although in this text it is not properly and exactly given as a rule) more strict than the moral precepts of the Decalogue itself, in which, as in all rules, there are naturally included and incorporated some exceptions. If they allow exceptions to this one, they are still at the beginning, for the case of self-homicide may itself fall within those exceptions.

Otherwise, the general application of this rule is improper. As from infinite other texts it appears evident from the passage in Bellarmine where he says that by reason of this rule a man may not adorn a church by neglecting a poor neighbor. Still, there are a great many cases in which we may neglect this poor neighbor, and therefore to do so is not naturally evil. Surely whoever is delighted with such arguments and such an application of this text would not only have called to Lot's attention this rule when (Gen. 19:6-8) he offered his daughters (for there it might have color), but also would have joined with Judas when the woman anointed Christ (Mark 14:3-11, John 12:3-7) and would have told her that although the office that she did was good yet the waste that she first made was evil and against this rule.

4. The same apostle in various other texts uses this phrase, "We are the temples of the Holy Ghost." From this it is argued that to demolish or to deface those temples is an unlawful sacrifice. But we are the temples of God in the same way that we are his images; that is, by his residing in our hearts. Who may doubt that the blessed souls of the departed are still his temples and images? Even among heathens those temples that were consecrated to their gods might be demolished in cases of public good or harm, and still the ground remained sacred.

In the first two texts (II Cor. 6:16 and I Cor. 3:16) there is only an exhortation against polluting our hearts, which are God's temples, with idolatry or other sin. In the other text (I Cor. 6:16) he calls our material body the temple, and he makes it an argument to us that we should flee from fornication, because therein we trespass against our own body. There arises here a double argument, that we may not do injury to our own bodies either as it is our own or as it is God's.

In the first of these he says, "A fornicator sins against his body," for, as he said two verses before, "He makes himself one body with a harlot," and thus he diminishes the dignity of his own person. But is this so in our case?—when he withdraws and purges his body from all corruptions and delivers it from all the pollutions, venom, and malign machinations of his (and God's) adversaries and prepares it by God's inspiration and concurrence for the glory that, without death, cannot be attained!

Is it a lesser dignity that one be the priest of God or the sacrifice of God than that one be the temple of God? Says Paul, "Your body is the temple of God, and you are not your own" (I Cor. 6:19). But Calvin on this point says that you are not your own in that you may live according to your own will or abuse your body with pollutions and uncleanness. Our body is so much our own that we may use it to God's glory, and it is so little our own that when he is pleased to have it we do well in resigning it to him, by whatever officer he accepts it, whether by angel, sickness, persecution, magistrate, or ourselves. Just be careful of this last lesson, in which Paul amasses and gathers together all his previous doctrine: "Glorify God in your body and in your spirit, for they are his" (I Cor. 6:20).

5. The text in Ephesians 4:15-16, "But let us follow the truth in love and in all things grow up into him who is the head, that is, Christ, until we are all come together into a perfect man," has some affinity with this one. By this we receive the honor to be one body with Christ our head, which is afterward more expressly declared, "We are members of his body, of his flesh, and of his bone" (Eph. 5:30). Therefore, they say that to withdraw ourselves, who are the limbs of him, is not only homicide of ourselves, who cannot live without him, but a parricide towards him who is our common father.

However, as in fencing passion lays a man as open as unskillfulness, and a troubled desire to hit makes him not only miss but also receive a wound, so he who alleges this text overreaches to his own danger. For only this is taught here: all our growth and vegetation flows from our head, Christ, who has chosen for himself, to perfect his body, limbs proportional to it, and as a soul must live through all the body so it, and as a soul must live through all the body so must this care live and dwell in every part, always ready to do its proper function and also to succor those other parts for whose relief or sustenance it is framed and planted in the body. Thus no literal construction is to be admitted here, as though the body of Christ could be damaged by the removal of any man. As some leaves pass their natural course and season and fall again from the tree, being withered with age, and some fruits are gathered unripe and some ripe, and some branches that fall off in a storm are carried to the fire, so in this body of Christ, the church—I mean that which is visible—all these are also fulfilled and performed, and yet the body suffers no maims, much less the head any detriment.

This text, then, is so far from giving encouragement to any particular man to be careful of his own well-being as the expositors, of whatever persuasion in controverted points, take from the text an argument that, for establishing and sustaining the whole body, a man is bound to dismiss all concerns for himself and give his life to strengthen those who are weak. This text as a common fountainhead has afforded justification for martyrdoms, for visiting those under pestilence, and for all those desertions of ourselves and of our natural right of preserving ourselves that we heretofore had occasion to insist upon.

6. Just as that construction consists well with those words, so does it also with the words in the next chapter, "No man ever hated his own flesh but nourished it, etc." (Eph. 5:2–9). Because we are to speak of this hate when we come to Christ's commandment about hating our life, here we will only say with Marlorat on this text, "He does not hate his flesh who hates its desires and would subject it to the spirit, any more than a goldsmith hates the gold that he casts into a furnace to purify and reduce to a better fashion."

Since I have not found that they take from the armory of scripture any more or better weapons than these, we may here end this distinction.

Distinction IV

1. In the next distinction our business is to test of what force and proof their arms are against their adversary forces. We shall oppose two kinds of them. The first are natural and assured subjects, reasons arising naturally from texts of scripture. The other, as auxiliaries, are examples. For although we do not rely upon them, still we have the advantage that our adversaries can neither use nor profit from examples! Therefore, the answer that both Peter Martyr and Lavater, borrowing from him, make— that we must not live by examples and that if examples proved anything they would have the stronger side (after all, there have been more men who have not killed themselves than who have done so—may well seem peremptory or lazy and the impossibility of a better defense may seem to be so alloyed as to be irrelevant. To prepare us for a right understanding and application of these texts from scripture, we must linger a while on the nature, degrees, and effects of charity, the mother and form of all virtue, which not only will lead us to heaven (for faith opens the door for us) but also will continue with us when we are there, when both faith and hope are spent and useless.

Nowhere will we find a better portrait of charity than the one Saint Augustine has drawn: she does not love that which should not be loved, and she does not neglect that which should be loved; she does not bestow more love upon that which deserves less love, nor does she equally love more and less worthiness; she does not bestow upon equal worthiness more and less love. To this charity the same blessed and happy Father apportions this growth. "Initiated, increased, grown great, and perfected—and the last is," he says, "when in regard for it we hate this life." Still, he acknowledges a higher charity than this one. For Peter the Lombard allows charity this growth: "Beginning, proficient, perfect, more perfect, and most perfect." He cites Saint Augustine who calls it "Perfect charity to be ready to die for another." But when he comes to that than which none can be greater, he says the apostle came "To desire to depart this life and be with Christ" (Phil. 1:23).

So, "One may love God with all his heart, and yet he may grow and love God more with all his heart, for the first was commanded in the law, and yet the counsel of perfection was given to him who said that he had fulfilled the first commandment." Just as Saint Augustine found a degree above charity, which made a man ready to offer life, which is to desire to depart and be with Christ, so there is a degree above that, which is to do it.

This is the virtue by which martyrdom, which is not such in itself, becomes an act of highest perfection. This is the virtue too that assures any suffering that proceeds from it to be infallibly accompanied by the grace of God. Upon the assurance and testimony of a rectified conscience that we have a charitable purpose, let us consider how far we may adventure on the authority of scripture in this matter that we have in hand.

2. To begin with, look at the frame and working of Saint Paul's argument to the Corinthians, "Though I give my body to be burned, and have not charity, it profits me nothing" (I Cor. 13:3). Two things seem evident. First, in a general notion and common reputation it was counted a high degree of perfection to die so, and therefore it was not counted against the law of nature. Second, by this exception, "without charity," with love it might be done well and profitably.

As for the first, if anybody thinks the apostle here takes an example of an impossible thing, as when it is said, "If an angel from heaven teach another doctrine" (Gal. 1:8), he will, I believe, correct himself if he considers the foregoing verses and the apostle's progress in his argument. In order to dignify charity the most that he can, he undervalues all other gifts, which there were ambitiously liked. As for eloquence, he says it is nothing to have all languages, even that of the angels (I Cor. 13:1). This is not put literally, since angels have no language, but to express a high degree of eloquence, as Calvin says on this point; or, according to Nicholas of Lyra, by language is meant the desire of communicating our ideas to one another. Then Paul adds that a knowledge of mysteries and prophesies, which also was much liked, is also nothing (I Cor. 13:2). The same for miraculous faith; it is also nothing.

The first of these gifts does not make a man better, for Balaam's ass could speak (Num. 22:30) and still was an ass. The second gift Judas and the Pharisees had. The third gift is so small a matter that as much as a grain of mustard seed (Matt. 17:20) is enough to remove mountains. All these were feasible things and were sometimes done. After he had passed through the gifts of knowledge and the gifts of utterance, he presents the gifts of good works in the same stages. Therefore, he says, "If I feed the poor with all my goods" (I Cor. 13:3), which he presents as a harder thing than either of the others because in the others God gives to me but here I give to the other, yet as a thing possible to be done. Then he presents the last, "If I give my body," as the hardest of all and yet, like all the rest, sometimes to be done.

What I observed as arising secondly from this argument was that with charity such a death might be acceptable. I know that the Donatists are said to have made this use of these words. Still, the intent and the aim condition every action and infuse the poison or the nourishment that those who follow suck from it. The Donatists rigorously and tyrannously racked and extorted so much from this text, in order to present themselves to others to be promiscuously killed, and if that were denied them they might kill themselves as well as those who refused to kill them. Still, I say, I do not doubt that so much may be gathered from this text as by these words, "If I give my body" (I Cor. 13:3), is implied rather more than a prompt and willing yielding of it when I am forced to do so by the persecuting magistrate.

These words will justify the deed of the martyr Nicephorus, being then in perfect charity. His case was this. Having some enmity with Sapricius, who was brought to the place where he was to receive the bloody crown of martyrdom, he fell down to Sapricius and begged from him a pardon of all former bitternesses. Sapricius, elated with the glory of martyrdom, refused him but was soon punished. His faith cooled and he lived. Nicephorus, standing by, stepped into his place and cried, "I am also a Christian," and so provoked the magistrate to execute him, lest from the faintness of Sapricius the cause might have received a wound or a scorn. I take this to be a giving of his body.

Where there is a necessity to confirm weaker Christians it is very probable, as in this case, that a man may be bound to commit self-homicide. So there may be cases in which a very exemplary man before a prosecutor of cunning and subtle carriage can in no other way give his body for testimony to God's truth, to which he may then be bound, except by doing it himself.

3. Since men naturally and customarily thought it good to die by self-homicide, and that such a death with charity was acceptable, so it is generally said by Christ, "The good shepherd gives his life for his sheep" (John 10:11). This is a justification and approval of our inclination to do so. For to say that the good do it is to say that they who do it are good!

Since we all are sheep of one fold, so in many cases we all are shepherds of one another and owe one another this duty of giving our temporal lives for another's spiritual advantage, even for his temporal advantage. That I may abstain from purging myself when another's crime is imputed to me is grounded in another text such as this one, where it is said, "The greatest love is to bestow his life for his friend" (John 15:13). In this matter and all of its kind we must remember that we are commanded to do as Christ did. How Christ gave his body we shall have to consider below.

4. On these grounds, Saint Peter's zeal was so forward and carried him so high that he wanted to die for the shepherd, for he says, "I will lay down my life for your sake" (John 13:37). All expositors say this was merely and purely out of natural affection, without examination of his own strength to do it, but soon nature carried him fully to that promise. In a more deliberate and orderly resolution Saint Paul testifies of himself, "I will gladly be spent for your souls" (II Cor. 12:15).

5. A Christian nature does not rest in knowing that we may do it, that charity makes it good, that the good do it, and that we must always promise (that is, incline) to do it and do something towards it. A Christian nature will have the prefect fulness of doing it in the resolution, doctrine, and example of our blessed savior, who said, in fact, "I lay down my life for my sheep" (John 10:15). He used the present tense, says Musculus, because he was ready to do it, just as Paul and Barnabas, while still alive, are said to have laid down their lives for Christ. But I rather think that, because exposing oneself to danger is not properly called dying, Christ said this at that time because his passion had begun. All his doings here were steps toward laying down his life.

All words are defective to express the abundant and overflowing charity of our savior, for if we could express all that he did, even that would not come near to what he would do if need be. It is observed by Malloni—I confess too credulous an author, yet one who administers good and wholesome incitements to devotion—that Christ going to Emmaus spoke of his passion so slightly, as though he had in three days forgotten all that he had suffered for us.

Christ in an apparition to Saint Charles says that he would be content to die again, if need be. Yes, to Saint Bridgit he said that "For any one soul he would suffer as much in every limb as he had suffered for all the world in his whole body." It is noted as an extremely high degree of charity, according to Anselm, that Christ's blessed mother said, "Rather than he should not have been crucified, she would have done it with her own hands." Certainly his charity was not inferior to hers. He did as much as any could be willing to do.

As he himself said, "No man can take away my soul," and, "I have power to lay it down" (John 10:18). Without doubt, no man took it away, nor was there any other cause of his dying at that time than his own will, for many martyrs have hanged alive upon crosses for many days, and the thieves were still alive, and therefore Pilate marveled to hear that Christ was so soon dead. "His soul," says Saint Augustine, "did not leave his body under constraint but because he willed it to happen and he willed when and how it happened." Of this Saint Thomas Aquinas produced this sign, that he still had his body's nature in its full strength, because at the last moment he was able to cry with a loud voice. Marlorat gathers that whereas our heads decline after our death by the slackness of the sinews and muscles, Christ first on his own bowed down his head and then gave up the ghost. Although it is truly said, "After they have scourged him, they will put him to death" (Luke 18:33), yet it is said thus because, maliciously and purposely to kill him, they inflicted upon him those pains that in time would have killed him. But nothing that they had done occasioned his dying so quickly.

Therefore Aquinas, a man neither of unholy thoughts nor of bold, irreligious, or scandalous phrase or elocution (still, I do not venture so far in his behalf as Mazzolini does, that "It is impossible that he should have spoken any things against faith or good manners"), does not stop short of saying that "Christ was so much the cause of his death as one is of his own wetting who might but would not shut the window when the rain beats in."

This actual emitting of his soul is his death and was his own act, before his natural time. His best-loved apostle could imitate it who also died when he would and went into his grave and there buried himself, which is reported of only a very few others, and by not very credible authors. We find Christ's emitting of his own soul thus celebrated: "That is a brave death which is accepted unconstrained, and that is a heroic act of fortitude if a man, when an urgent occasion is presented, exposes himself to a certain and assured death, as he did."

It is said that Christ did just as Saul did, who thought it foul and dishonorable to die by the hand of an enemy. Also it is said that Apollonia and others who anticipated the fury of executioners and cast themselves into the fire were imitating this act by our savior of giving up his soul before he was constrained to do it. Therefore, if the act of our blessed savior, for whom there was no more required for death but that he should will that his soul depart, was the same as Saul's and these martyrs' actual helping further their own deaths (without which they could not have died), then we are taught that all those texts about "Giving up our bodies to death" and "Laying down the soul" signify more than yielding to death when it comes.

6. As I understand it, there is a further degree of cheerful readiness and proneness to such a death expressed in the phrase of John 12:25, "He who hates his life in this world shall keep it in life eternal"; also, in that of Luke 14:26, "Unless he hates his own life, he cannot be my disciple." Such a loathing to live is what is spoken of in Hebrews 12:35, "Some were racked and would not be delivered, so that they might receive a

better resurrection." Calvin interprets John 12:25 as a readiness to die and expresses it elegantly as carrying our life in our own hands and offering it to God for a sacrifice. The Jesuits in their rule extend the matter this far, "Let everyone think that this was said directly to him, 'Hate your life.'"

Those who, on the other hand, stand by this phrase, "No man hates his own flesh" (Eph. 5:29) must, to yield an argument against self-homicide in every case, also allow that the hate that is commanded here authorizes that act in some cases. Saint Augustine, apprehending the strength of this text, denies that by its authority the Donatists can justify their self-homicide when they wish to die. Still, in those cases that are exempt from his rules, this text may encourage a man not to neglect the honor of God for the sole reason that nobody else will take his life.

7. The Holy Ghost proceeds more directly in the First Epistle of Saint John 3:16 and shows us a necessary duty, "Because he laid down his life for us, therefore we ought to lay down our lives for our brethren." All these texts bring us to a true understanding of charity and to a contempt of this life in respect of charity.

As these texts inform us how ready we must be, so all the texts that direct us by the example of Christ to do as he did show that, in cases when our lives must be given up, we need not always wait for extrinsic force by others but, as he did in perfect charity so we in such degrees of it as this life and our nature are capable of, we must die by our own will rather than let his glory be neglected, whenever, as Paul says, Christ may be magnified in our bodies (Phil. 1:20), or the spiritual good of another whose good we are bound to advance importunes it.

8. To this readiness of dying for his brethren Saint Paul had so accustomed himself and made it his nature that, except for his general resolution of always doing what would promote their happiness, he could hardly have obtained for himself permission to live. At first he says he did not know which to wish for, life or death. Therefore, unless some circumstance inclines or averts us, life and death are generally equal to our nature. Then, after much perplexity, he made up his mind, and he desired to be released and to be with Christ. Therefore, a holy man may wish it. Still, he corrected that again, because he says, "For me to abide in the flesh is more needful for you" (Phil. 1:24). Therefore, charity must be the rule of our wishes and actions in this matter.

9. Another text, Galatians 4:15, although it does not extend to death, proves that holy men may be ready to express their loves to others by violence to themselves: "If it had been possible, you would have plucked out your own eyes and given them to me." Calvin says, "This was more than to pour out one's life." Saint Paul does not reprehend this readiness in them.

10. The highest degree of compassionate charity for others is that of the apostle in contemplating the Jews' dereliction, "I would wish myself

to be separated from Christ for my brethren's sake" (Rom. 9:3).

The bitterness of this damnation he himself teaches us to understand when in another place he wishes the same "To those who do not love Jesus Christ" (I Cor. 16:22). This fearful wish that charity excused in him was utter damnation, as all the expositors say. Although I believe with Calvin that at this time, in a zealous fury, he deliberately did not remember his own election and therefore cannot in that respect be said to have resisted the will of God, still it remains as an argument to us that charity will recompense and justify many excesses that appear to be unnatural, irregular, and enormous ecstasies.

11. As in the apostle to the gentiles so in the law-giver of the Jews, the same compassion worked the same result—and more. Moses did not rest in wishing but argued face to face with God, "If you pardon them, your mercy shall appear, but if you will not, I pray you to blot my name out of the book that you have written" (Exod. 32:32).

I know that many, out of a reasonable idea that it became Moses to be reposed, dispassionate, and of temperate affections in his conversation with God, are of the opinion that he strayed no further in this wish and imprecation than to be content that his name be blotted out of the scriptures and so to lose the honor of being known to posterity as a remarkable instrument of God's power and mercy. But since a natural infirmity could work so much upon Christ—in whom we may suspect no inordinateness of affections to divert him a little and make him slip a faint wish of escaping the cup (Matt. 26:39)—why might not a brave and noble zeal exalt Moses enough to desire to restore his nation to the love of God by his own destruction? As certainly as the first of these was without sin, so the other might be out of a habitual assuredness of his salvation. As Paulinus says to Amandus, "You may be bold in your prayers to God for me and say, 'Forgive him, or blot me out,' for you cannot be blotted out; justice cannot blot out the just." Always keeping in our minds that our example is Christ and that he died unconstrained, it will suffice to have learned from these texts that in charity men may so die, have so done, and ought so to do.

The last thing that remains is to consider the examples reported in the scriptures. That cannot keep us long, because a few rules will include many examples, and the few rules that are applicable to these stories have already often been gone over. Other rules that may enlighten and govern us in all occurrences I postpone for many reasons to a maturer deliberation and discourse.

Distinction V

1. When I entered into the examination of texts from scripture, it seemed to me to have some weight that in all the judicial and ceremonial

law there was no abomination of self-homicide. Just so, in relating the stories of those who killed themselves, the phrases of scripture never put them down by any aspersion or imputation for that act if they were otherwise virtuous, nor does it aggravate for that reason their former wickedness if they were wicked.

For my part, I am content to submit myself to the rule that is delivered by Irenaeus, "It does not become us to attack those things that the scripture does not reprehend but simply lays down, nor should we make ourselves more diligent than God; but if anything seems to us irregular, our endeavor must be to search out its type and signification."

Nor shall I, for all of this, be in the danger of Beza's answer to the argument of Ochino that some of the patriarchs lived unreprehended in polygamy. This is inconclusive, answered Beza, because the scripture is silent about Jacob's (Gen. 29:21–30) and Lot's (Gen. 19:30–38) incest and about David's unjust judgment (II Sam. 11); but Ziba did not absolve them from guilt and transgression in these acts (I Sam. 9, 16, 19). Our case differs from all others, first, because this act of self-homicide is not shown to be sin by any text of the law, and second, because there is a concurrence of examples of this act without any reprehension. Thus Beza's answer falls as far short from reaching us as it fell in not reaching home to the argument of Ochino against which it was opposed. If in debating these examples it is found that some very reverend authors have concluded a lack of repentance by self-homicide, and therefore utter desertion by God, and thus eternal perishing, then the circumstances as they appeared to that author then may have made his judgment just. But for anybody else to apply that case to others will not be safe. For according to Ennenckel, "Although a judge by reason of circumstances may interpret the law, that interpretation does not make law."

2. Just as in the former distinctions we spoke of some approaches to the act of self-killing, so in this one we will pause briefly on two such steps. The first is the prophet "Who bade a stranger to strike him. Because the stranger would not, he pronounced a heavy judgment that was soon executed. Then he importuned another to strike him, who did it thoroughly, wounding him with a stroke" (I Kgs. 20:35). To the common understanding this was an unnatural thing that so holy a man would take such means to have his body violated. It seems that the first stranger so understood it, but it pleased God to enlighten the second one. This I bring forth not as though the prophet inclined to it of his own disposition, for it is expressly in the text that God commanded him to do it.

But since this is the only place in all the scriptures where those who offer or desirously admit violence to their own bodies are said to have done it by the express motion of God, I gather that it is not without some boldness that others affirm, without the authority of the text, that the death of Samson and others had the same foundation, for it appears by this that when God would have it thus understood he is pleased to speak it plainly and expressly.

3. Before we come to those who actually killed themselves, the next is Jonah 1:12. By frequently wishing his own death and moving the mariners to cast him into the sea, Jonah made many steps toward the very act. I know that it is everywhere said that these words, "Take me and cast me into the sea," proceeded from a prophetic spirit. Saint Jerome says, "In this prophetic spirit he foresaw that the Ninevites would repent, and so his preaching would be discredited." But if this is so, must he not also in the same prophetic spirit see that their repentance must be occasioned by his going there and preaching? If this request for his own destruction—they were then innocent in their understanding, for they prayed, "Lay not innocent blood upon us" (Jonah 1:14)—was by divine motion, shall we dare also to impute to similar motions and spirit his angry importuning of death? "Take, I beseech you, my life from me, for it is better for me to die than to live" (Jonah 4:3). Then, after he wished in his heart to die, he added, "I do well to be angry unto the death" (Jonah 4:9).

Saint Jerome calls him "Saint Jonah." When Nicholas of Lyra observes that Jerome had not done so to any of the other prophets, he concludes that this testimony was most needed by Jonah, who by his many reluctances against God's will might otherwise fall into some suspicion of eternal perishing. We must be far from fearing such a fate in so eminent and exemplary a type of Christ. But we have no ground to admit any particular inspiration of God's spirit, since Jerome and Nicholas of Lyra pronounce him holy, despite all of these reluctances. Thus we may esteem him advised, ordinate, and rectified in all these approaches that he made by wishing for and consenting to his own death.

4. Samson is the first of those whom the scriptures register to have killed themselves. The man is so exemplary! The times before him prophesied him, for of him it is said, "Dan shall judge his people" (Gen. 49:16). The times after him regarded him more consummately in Christ, of whom he was a figure. Even in his own times other nations seem to have had a type or copy of him in Hercules. His act of self-killing is celebrated by the church to everlasting memory as the act of a martyr, and by very many others in their homilies and expositions. The renowned Paulinus says, "God send me the death of Samson and Samson's blindness, that I may live to God and look to God."

This general applause and concurrence in praising the act has made many, being loath either to depart from their opinion who extol him or to admit anything that may countenance that manner of dying, think (or at least write) that he did not intend to kill himself. Two very learned men, Francisco de Vitoria and Gregorio de Valencia, labor to seem to be of this persuasion. Beside the fact that exposing himself thus to inevitable danger is the same fault as self-homicide, when there is any fault in it, the text itself is against them. For Samson died with these words in his mouth, "Let me lose my life with the Philistines" (Judges 16:30).

These authors sometimes add that he intended his own death not principally but only accidentally. (Calvin also says that Saint Paul did not desire death for death's sake but to be with Christ.) This, however, can remove no man from our side of the argument, for we say the same, that this may be done only when the honor of God may be promoted in that way and no other.

Therefore, to justify Samson's act, Saint Augustine, equally zealous of Samson's honor and of his own conscience, still builds on his old foundation, "This was by special inspiration from God." Because it does not appear in the story explicitly or implicitly, this may be refuted as easily as it is presented. To give strength to this opinion of Augustine, our countryman Sayer presents one reason preceding the act. Pedraza the Spaniard gives another reason subsequent to the act. The first is that he prepared himself for it by prayer. But in this prayer you may observe much humanity, weakness, and self-regard. "O Lord," says he, "I beseech you, strengthen me alone at this time, that I may be avenged of the Philistines for my two eyes" (Judges 16:28). The second reason is that, because he effected what he desired, it is to be presumed that to the end for which he asked it God restored his strength to him.

In the text it appears that already his hair had begun to grow out again, and thus his strength was somewhat renewed. But does this prove any impulse, incitement, and prevenience of the holy God to that particular act, or rather only a habitual accompanying and awakening of him to such actions by which God might be honored and glorified, whenever an occasion was presented? Therefore, when he felt his strength in part refreshed and had by prayer entreated the perfecting of it, seeing that they took continual occasion from his dejection to scorn and reproach his God, Samson turned with an equal fervor to revenge their offense against him and God, and to remove the wretched occasion of it.

A very subtle author, Georgius, says Samson had the same reason to kill himself that he had to kill them, the same authority, the same privilege, and the same safeguard from sin. He died, the same man says, with the same zeal as Christ, unconstrained. Writes Pereira, "In this manner of dying, as much as in anything else, he was a type of Christ."

5. The next example is Saul. Whether he performed and consummated the act of killing himself or the Amalekite contributed his help makes no difference to our purpose. That the latter was true may consist well enough with the first telling of the story in I Samuel 31, and it appears to be the more likely and probable in the second telling in II Samuel 1. By Josephus it is absolutely so declared. Peter Comestor's *Scholastic History* also says that Saul was too weak to force the sword through his body.

Two things used to be disputed about Saul—whether or not he was saved and whether if he perished it was for impenitence either testified or presumed by this act of his. The Jews are generally indulgent toward him. The Christians are generally severe for the reason that it is said of him, "Saul died for his transgressions against the Lord and his word and for asking counsel of a witch" (I Chron. 10:13). This does not necessarily indicate an impenitence or a second death of damnation. For the Jews say that he, believing the sentence of Samuel (I Sam 28:16) in the apparitions and accepting that decree as from God, repented his former life, and then presented and delivered up himself and his sons, conformably to the revealed will of God, there in the field to be sacrificed to him. That is to understand Samuel's words, "You shall be with me," to be spoken not generally of the state of the dead but of the state of the just, because both Samuel himself was just and so was Jonathan, whose condition in this promise of being with Samuel was the same as his father's.

Nicholas of Lyra says, "All Jews and some Christians agree that, lest by his reproach dishonor might redound upon God, a good and zealous man may kill himself, as Samson and the virgins did." He adds, "If other reasons were not sufficient to excuse Saul, it also might justly be applied to him that he did it by divine inspiration." From these statements I observe two things. First, Nicholas presumes there are other reasons that are sufficient in some cases, whether or not they were there in Saul's case. Second, there is the reason for which Nicholas presumes that Saul died well, "Because the contrary is not declared in scriptures nor determined by the church."

Saul, indeed, has a good testimony of sanctity in this act from Malloni: "As Christ died when he would, so did Saul, thinking it dishonorable to die by the hand of his and God's enemies." The argument that Paul of Burgos makes to the contrary suffers more force and violence in being brought in than it gives strength to his opinion; it is, "If the act were justifiable in Saul, it would have been so too in the Amalekite, if his profession to David was true that he had killed Saul, and consequently David was unjust in that execution." Besides that, the Amalekite had no consciousness or inward knowledge of Saul's just reasons, nor any other warrant except his commandment. It might have, and to him seemed likely to have, proceeded from Saul's infirmities, and it might well appear to David from the Amalekite's coming to tell him the news that he had human concerns in doing it and a purpose only to deserve well of David. When both judge and prisoner are innocent, often the executioner may be a murderer.

Such human concerns as weariness, despair, shame, fear, fidelity to his master, amazement, and so forth, stand in the way between Saul's armor-bearer and all the excuses in our understandings. Although the phrase of scripture imputes nothing to him for the fact that he killed himself, still I have found nobody who offers any particular excuse in his defense.

6. Neither do I find anything to excuse Ahitophel's death (II Sam. 17:23), although, as I said of the other one, the story does not condemn that particular act. The text calls his counsel good, and it seems that he was not transported with passion, because he set his house in order, and he was buried in his father's grave when Absalom, slain by another's hand, was cast into a pit (II Sam. 18:14–17). But if he did it over a mere dispute of his own disgrace, or from fear of failure, or out of any self-concern, without advancing God's glory, and he did not repent, then he perished.

7. The usual (though not universal) opinion of Judas, the most sinful instrument of the most merciful work, is that he killed himself, but whether or not by hanging is more debated.

From the words in Acts 1:18, "He threw himself down headlong and burst asunder, and his bowels gushed out," Euthymius thinks that while he hanged he was rescued and carried away, and that afterwards he killed himself by throwing himself headlong. Brenz leaves it neutral for us to think what we will. Oecumenius says that he did not only outlive this hanging but also grew to so enormous a size and became such a burden to himself that he was not able to get himself out of a coach's way and so had his guts crushed out. Oecumenius got this from Papias, the disciple of Saint John, whose times cannot be thought ignorant or incurious of Judas's story. There it is further told that others said Judas, being swollen to that vastness and corrupted with vermin, laid himself down in his field, and there his guts broke out. This version Theophylact follows.

It happens very often that some particular Father, of strong reputation and authority in his own time, snatches and swallows some probable interpretation of scripture. Then he digests it into his homilies, applies it in exhortations and encouragements as the diseases of his audience or his age require, imagines in it delightful and figurative insinuations, and sets it to the music of his style. In fact, every man who is accustomed to these meditations will often find in himself such a spiritual wantonness and devout straying into such delicacies. Then the sense that was only probable grows to be necessary, and those who follow that Father would rather enjoy his wit than exercise their own, just as we are often loath to change or remove a counterfeit gem by reason of its fine setting. In this way, I think, it became so widely believed that the fruit Eve ate was an apple, that Lot's wife was turned into a pillar of salt, that Absalom was hanged by the hair of the head, that Jephthah killed his daughter, and many others that grew current not from evidence in the text but because such an interpretation was most useful and applicable.

Judas's case may well belong to this number. If not, still the act of killing himself is not added to his faults in any scriptural text, not even in those two Psalms (69, 109) that are commonly taken to be prophetically intended and directed as particular accusations against him.

Origen dared to hope even for this man (whose sin exceeded mercy if any ever did so), not out of Origen's erroneous compassion and sinful charity by which he thinks that even the devil will be saved, but by virtue of Judas's repentance. He says, "The devil led him to the sin and then induced in him the sorrowfulness that swallowed him." But speaking of Judas's repentance, he says, "Those words, 'when Judas saw that he was condemned' (Matt. 27:3), apply to Judas himself, for Christ was not yet condemned. From this consciousness and consideration began his repentance." Origen also says, "It may be that Satan, who had entered into him, stayed with him until Christ was betrayed and then left him, and thereafter repentance followed. Perhaps," Origen goes on, "he went to precede and go before his master, who was to die, and to meet him with his naked soul, so he might gain mercy by his confession and prayers."

Although Calvin's purpose is to enervate and maim (or at least to declare defective) the repentance that is admitted as sufficient by the Roman Church, he says that "in Judas there was perfect contrition of heart, confession by the mouth, and satisfaction for the money." But Petilianus, against whom Saint Augustine wrote, proceeded further than any in justifying Judas's last act. He said, "In suffering death when he repented, and thus was a confessor, he became a martyr." This opinion, pronounced singularly and indefensibly, Saint Augustine answers just as cholerically, "He left to such a noose" [i.e., Judas left a noose for the likes of Petilianus]. Even so, Saint Augustine himself confesses that an innocent man would have sinned more in such an act than Judas did, because in his execution there were some degrees of justice.

I intended not to speak of his actual impenitence or of his repentance, but only to observe to you that this last act is not imputed to him, nor is repentance said to be precluded by it.

8. Nobody denies the passive action of Eleazar, but they hold that the endangering of himself was an act of virtue. Still it was a forsaking and exposing of himself to certain destruction (I Macc. 6:43–46). For every elephant had thirty-two men on him and was guarded by 1,000 foot-soldiers and 500 horsemen; the elephant he slew was in his opinion the king's and therefore the better provided. Even if prior to killing the elephant he hoped to escape, his creeping under it was a direct killing of himself, as expressly as Samson's pulling down the house. The reasons for this action are rendered in the text to have been to deliver his people and to earn a perpetual name.

Saint Ambrose extols this act by many glorious circumstances; for instance, "That he flung away his shield, which might have sheltered him, so that, despising death, he forced his way into the midst of the army." Also, "Being hemmed in rather than overwhelmed by catastrophe, he was buried in his triumph." Again, "By death he begat peace as the heir of his valor."

Very many scholastics have stretched and exercised their wits in praise of this action. Cajetan gives a reason for it that as is applicable to very many self-homicides: "To expose ourselves to certain death, if our first aim is not our own death but the common good, is lawful. For," he says, "our actions that may be morally good or bad must be judged to be such by the reason that first motivates them, not by any accident, concomitance, accompaniment, or succeeding of them, although necessarily." This decision of Cajetan's will include many cases and instances that are condemned headlongly by intemperate censures.

9. The fall of Razis, our last example, is reported as follows. "He was beseiged and set afire. Willing to die manfully and to escape reproach that would be unworthy of his house, he fell upon his sword. In haste, he missed his first stroke and threw himself from the castle wall. Still, he got up again and ran to a high rock, took out his own bowels, and threw them among the people, calling upon the Lord of life and spirit. So he died" (II Macc. 14:41–46 excerpted).

This act the text does not accuse. Saint Thomas Aquinas accuses it of nothing except cowardliness, which Aristotle also imputes to this manner of dying, as we said before. Either Aquinas then spoke serviceably and advantageously to the point that he had in hand, or else he spoke for the most part, because for the most part infirmities provoke men to this act.

Saint Augustine, who argued as earnestly as Aristotle that this act is not one of greatness of mind, confesses that it was just that in Cleombrotus who, simply upon reading Plato's *Phaedo*, killed himself. Said Augustine, "When no calamity urged him, no crime either true or imputed, nothing but greatness of mind moved him to apprehend death and to break the sweet bands of this life." To be sure, he added that "It was done rather greatly than well." But we now are seeking only the concession that sometimes there is in this act greatness and courage. What moved Aristotle and all the rest to be loath to cite too many cases was to quench in men their natural love of self-homicide.

For Augustine says, "Except for Lucrecia, it is not easy to find any example worth prescribing or imitating—except Cato, not only because he did it but because, being reputed learned and honest, men might justly think that what he did was well done and might well be done again." For all this, he is loath to let Cato's act pass with much approbation, for he adds, "Yet many of his learned friends thought it a weakness to let him die thus." He adds it because, when men have before them the precedent of a brave example, they do not ask further than *what* he did—not *why* he did it.

It is truly said, "Examples do not stop, nor do they consist in the degree where they began, but they grow, and no man thinks that what has profited another is unworthy for himself." Saint Augustine, for this reason loath to give glory to many examples, still allows all greatness and praise to Regulus, of whom we spoke before—even though, to my understanding, there are in this example many impressions of falsehood and of ostentation, from all of which Cato's story is free.

To conclude this point, whether it is always done from cowardliness, Diogenes Laertius says that "Antisthenes the philosopher seemed to show more weakness in that, lying extremely sick, and Diogenes asking him if he lacked a friend (meaning to kill him) and also offering his dagger to do it himself, the philosopher said he desired an end of pain but not of life."

Since the self-homicide of Razis may have proceeded from greatness, Nicholas of Lyra excused it from all sin, by reasons that are applicable to many others. He says, "Either to escape torment, by which a man might probably be seduced to idolatry, or to take away the occasion of making others reproach God in him, a man may kill himself, for both of these cases are ordained by God." Francisco de Vitoria allows this as the more probable opinion. Soto and Valencia follow Aquinas's opinion. Paul of Burgos condemns it on the presumption that he could not do it for the love of the common good, because the act could not redeem his people who were already captive. Paul of Burgos's accusing him helps our case in that, if by his death he could have redeemed them, he might lawfully have done it.

CONCLUSION

This is as far as I allowed my discourse to progress in this way, forbidding it earnestly all dark and dangerous withdrawals and diversions into points of our free will and God's destiny. Still, allowing many ordinary contingencies to be under choice, it may seem reasonable that our main periods—of birth, death, and major alterations—in this life are more immediately worked upon by God's determination. It is usefully said and applicable to good purpose (although by a wicked man, Muhammad, with the intention of crossing Moses) that "Man was made of shadow and the devil of fire." For as shadow is not darkness but grosser light, so is man's understanding in these mysteries not blind but clouded. As fire does not always give light (for fire is accidental and must have air to work upon) but burns naturally, so the desire of knowledge that the devil kindles in us—he as willingly bellows to inflame a heart curious of knowledge as he brings more ashes to stupify and bury deeper a slumbering understanding—does not always give us light. But fire always burns us and imprints upon our judgment stigmatic marks, and at least it sears up our conscience.

If the reasons that differ from me and my reasons are otherwise equal, still theirs have this disadvantage; they fight with themselves and suffer a civil war of contradiction. For many of their reasons incline us to a love of this life and a horror of death, and yet they say often that we are by nature too much addicted to all that. It is well noted by Alcuin (I think from Saint Augustine) that "Although there are four things that we must love, yet there is no precept given concerning more than two, God and our neighbor." Thus the others, which concern loving ourselves, may be omitted on some occasions.

Enough has been occasionally inserted above concerning the benefits of death. Having presented Cyprian's encouragement to it—who out of a contemplation that the whole frame of the world decayed and languished, cries to us, "The walls and the roof shake, and would you not go out? You are tired in a pilgrimage, and would you not go home?"—I shall end by applying to death, which deserves it better, Ausonius's thanks to the emperor, "You provide that your benefits and the good that you bring shall not be transitory and that the ills from which you deliver us shall never return." So, because death has a little bitterness, but medicinally, and a little alloy, but to make it more useful, they would utterly decline and avert our nature from it.

Paracelsus says of that foul, contagious disease [i.e., syphilis] that then had invaded mankind in a few places and has since overflowed into all places, God first inflicted that disease for the punishment of general licentiousness, and when the disease would not reduce us he sent a second and worse affliction, ignorant and torturing physicians. I may say the same of this case, that in punishment of Adam's sin God cast upon us an infectious death, and since then he has sent us a worse plague of men who accompany death with so much horror and fright that it can hardly be made wholesome and agreeable to us. They teach with too much liberty what Hippocrates admitted in cases of much profit and little danger, "Worse meat may be given to a patient, if it is pleasanter, and worse drink, if it is more acceptable."

I thought it needful to oppose this antidote—as much to encourage men toward a just contempt of this life and to restore them to their nature, which is a desire of supreme happiness in the next life through the loss of this one, as to rectify and wash again the frame of those who, religiously assuring themselves that in cases when we are destitute of other means, we might be to ourselves the stewards of God's benefits and the ministers of his merciful justice.

These persons, being innocent within themselves, as Ennodius said, had incurred injury of opinion. Still, as I said before, I abstained intentionally from extending this discourse to particular rules or instances, both because I dare not profess myself a master in so curious a science and because the limits of the subject are obscure, steep, slippery, and narrow, and also because every error is deadly, except where a competent diligence has been employed and a mistake of our conscience may provide an excuse.

The curing of diseases by touch or by charms is forbidden by various laws, even though one excellent surgeon (Paracelsus) and one excellent philosopher (Pomponazzi) are of the opinion that it may be done—because man, who is all, is capable of whatever virtue the heavens infuse into any creature, and, being sustained when that virtue is exacted, may receive a similar impression or may give it to a word or character made at that instant. Although this curing is forbidden by various laws, because of a just prejudice that vulgar owners of such a virtue would misuse it, still none objects that the kings of England and France should cure one sickness by such a means, nor that the kings of Spain should exorcise demon-possessed persons in this way, because kings are justly presumed to use all their power to the glory of God. So it is fitting that this privilege of which we speak should be contracted and restrained.

That is certainly true of what Cassian says of a lie, "It has the nature of [the herb] hellebore, wholesome in desperate diseases but otherwise poison," although I do not agree with him that, "We are in desperate diseases whenever we are in a state of great wealth or injury, and in humility to the shunning of vainglory." However, if Cassian mistakes that and we this, yet as he, Origen, Chrysostom, and Jerome are excused for following Plato's opinion that a lie might have the nature of medicine and be allowed in many cases (because in their time the church had not declared herself in that point nor pronounced that a lie was naturally evil), by the same reason I am excusable in this paradox.

If prejudice or contempt for my weakness or misdevotion has blocked any against the reasons for my case and against charity, such that they have not been pleased to taste and digest them, I must leave them to their drowsiness and bid them enjoy the favor of that indulgent physician, "Let him who cannot digest food sleep."

INDEX OF SCRIPTURAL REFERENCES

GLOSSARY OF NAMES

Abel, in Bible, second son of **Adam** and **Eve** who was murdered by his brother, Cain, 22

Abgar, 1st century, legendary king of Edessa, said by **Eusebius** to have exchanged letters with **Jesus**, 70

Abraham, in Bible, the traditional patriarch of the Jews and father of Isaac and Ishmael, 12, 53, 61

Absalom, in Bible, King **David**'s third son who murdered his brother Amnon and was killed by Joab in flight from battle, 6, 90

Acacius, see **Ennenckel, Georgius Acacius**

Acindynus, Septimius II, 4th century, a vicar of Spain under **Constantine I** and later a consul, 53

Adam, in Bible, the first person created by God, 49, 96

Ado of Vienne, 800?–875, French archbishop and historian, 63

Agapetus the Deacon, died 536, a member of an old Roman family who became pope in 535, 48

Agustín, Antonio, 1517–1586, Spanish humanistic scholar and bishop of Tarragon who supported reforms at the Council of **Trent** who wrote emendations to **Gratian**'s *Decretals*, 35

Ahitophel, in Bible, a counselor to King **David** who killed himself on the advice of **Absalom**, 90

Alcuin, 735–804, English scholar and educational leader at **Charlemagne**'s court, 95

Alfonso de Castro, 1495–1558, Spanish Franciscan theologian, influential at Council of **Trent**, who catalogued and refuted heresies from the beginning of Christianity to his own time, 28

Amandus, 7th century, French monk who missionized Belgium, 85

Ambrose of Milan, 340?–397, bishop of Milan and a Father of the church, 4, 12, 15, 48, 53, 63–64, 91

Anabaptists, 16th century and afterwards, literally the rebaptizers; various religious leaders and groups who rejected infant baptism for believer baptism, 71

Andrew, 1st century, one of **Jesus**' apostles who by tradition was martyred by crucifixion, 59

Anselm of Canterbury, 1033–1109, Italian-born scholastic theologian, Benedictine monk, and archbishop of Canterbury under King Henry I, 12, 82

Antisthenes, 444–after 371 BCE, Athenian philosopher who studied under **Socrates** and founded the Cynic school, 93

Antonius of Córdova, see **Córdoba, Antonio de**

Apollonia, died 249, an aged Christian deaconess who was martyred in Alexandria, 62–63, 83

Aquinas, Thomas, 1225?–1274, Italian-born Dominican theologian whose teachings became authoritative for the Roman Catholic Church, 8, 11, 12, 13, 14, 15, 16,

Bellarmine, Robert, 1542–1611, Italian **Jesuit** known for theological disputations against English and Scottish writers, 77

Bernardone, see **Francis of Assisi**

Bethsaida, in New Testament, a town on the Eastern bank of the Jordan River where there was a healing pool of running water, 4

Beza, Theodorus, 1519–1608, French Protestant theologian, co-worker and successor of **Calvin** as leader of the Reformation in Geneva, 3, 50, 68, 86

Binius, Severin, 1573–1641, German editor of Christian historical and conciliar texts, 36

Binsfeld, Pierre, 1540–1598, French Catholic pastoral and ascetical theologian, 61

Bodin, Jean, 1530–1596, French historian and political economist, 11

Bombastus, see **Paracelsus, Philippus Aureolus**

Bonarscius, see **Scribanius, Carolus**

Bonaventure, 1221–1271, Italian Franciscan philosopher and mystic, 53, 55

Bosquier, Philippe, 1562–1636, French Franciscan writer on the temptations of Christ in the desert, 3, 8, 54, 55

Bracton, Henry de, died 1268, English ecclesiastic and judge, author of first systematic treatise on medieval English laws, 37

Braga, Councils of, 563 and 572, church synods held in an ancient town in northern Portugal, important for adapting canon laws from the Greek church councils (Donne dated these councils after 590), 36–37

Brenz, Johann, 1499–1570, Lutheran reformer of Würtemberg, 90

Bridget of Sweden, 1303?–1373, founder of a female monastic order who dictated records of the revelations she received, 82

Brito, died 386, a bishop of Trèves in Gaul and opponent of an obscure heresy known as Priscillianism, 58

Bupalus, 6th century BCE, a sculptor who with a friend made a statue ridiculing the ugliness of the poet **Hipponax** who said that he lampooned them in verse until they were driven to hang themselves, 19

Buxtorf, Johann, 1564–1629, Swiss scholar of the Old Testament and of ancient Judaism, 40, 69

Caesar, Gaius Julius, 100–44 BCE, Roman general and statesman, conqueror of Gaul, 20

Cajetan, real name Tommaso de Vio, 1469–1534, Italian cardinal and papal legate (1518) at Augsburg who summoned Martin Luther before his tribunal, 12, 52, 92

Calvin, John, 1509–1564, French Protestant reformer of Geneva and biblical commentator, 8, 9, 15, 41, 43, 56, 74, 78, 80, 84, 85, 88, 91

Campion, Edmund, 1540–1581, English **Jesuit** missionary who was executed for treason, 4

Carbone, Lodovico, died 1597, Italian moral and dogmatic theologian of the Thomistic school, 28, 50

Cardan, Jerome, 1501–1576, Italian mathematician, physician, and astrologer, 18

Carthusian Order, 1084–, strictly contemplative monastic order founded in France by a monk named Bruno, 55

Casaubon, Isaac, 1559–1618, French classical scholar and humanist, 4

Cassian, John, 360?–?435, monk and theologian who traveled in Egypt and Palestine

Damocles, early 3rd century BCE, according to Plutarch a young Athenian of virtue and beauty who, pursued by Demetrius I into a private bathing room and seeing neither aid nor chance of escape, plunged himself into a cauldron of boiling water and died, 19

Dan, in Bible, the fifth son of **Jacob** and the ancestor of the tribe bearing his name, 87

David, 1039?–?973 BCE, in Bible, a king of Judah and Israel, anointed by **Samuel** as successor to **Saul,** 10, 57, 86, 89

Demosthenes, (385?–322 BCE), Athenian orator and statesman who took poison to avoid capture, 19

Depontans, cited by Donne as a people who legislated that sexagenarians take their lives by jumping from a bridge, 29

Diogenes Laertius, 3rd century, Greek biographer who wrote lives of philosophers, 19, 93

Domitian, 51–96, third member of the Flavian family to become an emperor of Rome, 19

Donatists, from early 4th century onwards into Middle Ages, Christians in North Africa who formed pietist churches and had courted martyrdom during persecutions under the Emperor Diocletian, 27, 81, 83

Donatus, early 5th century, a priest of the Donatist party in North Africa to whom **Augustine** addressed a letter in 416, 40, 62

Donne, John, 1604–1662, son and namesake of the poet; the publisher of *Biathanatos,* 1

Dorotheus of Gaza, 6th century, founder of a monastery who was famous for sermons to his monks on monastic virtue, 17, 38, 59

Draco, 7th century BCE, Athenian lawgiver who prescribed death for many offenses; thus "Draconian" came to mean harsh or cruel, 49

Duns Scotus, John, 1265?–1308, Scottish Franciscan friar and scholastic theologian, 38

Eleazar, Jewish scribe who, in II Maccabees 6:18–31, chose to be killed rather than to eat polluted food, 62, 91

Eleazar, died 70 CE, Jewish leader of revolt at Masada against Rome who, according to **Josephus,** led hundreds to their deaths rather than surrender to Rome, 20, 45

Elkesai or Elkasai, Elxai, Elcesai, 2nd century, name of the leader or of the scriptures of a Jewish–Christian sect akin to the Gnostics, later known as Ebionites or Sabians, 26

Emmanuel Sa, see **Sa, Manoel de**

Emmaus, in New Testament, a town in Palestine en route to which two of **Jesus'** disciples encountered him as resurrected, 82

Empedocles, 5th century BCE, Greek philosopher and statesman who, according to tradition, hurled himself into the flaming crater of Mount Etna, 27

Ennenckel, Georgius Acacius, baron von Hoheneck, also Enenckel, born 1573, a scholar of history, antiquity, and politics and expert on the laws of privileges, 15, 17, 52, 73, 86

Ennodius, Magnus Felix, 473?–521, a Roman Christian writer and bishop of Pavia, 96

Eugenius III, died 1153, pope who with his friend Bernard of Clairvaux promoted the Second Crusade, 35

Eunapius, born 347, Greek sophist and historian who was hostile to Christianity, 23

Euphemites, 4th century, admirers and followers of a legendary Christian virgin and martyr named Euphemia, 27

Euse, see **John XXII**

Eusebius Pamphili, 260?–?340, bishop of Caesarea and writer of ecclesiastical histories; biographer of **Constantine I,** 23, 25, 27, 63–64

Eusebius Hieronymus, see **Jerome**

Euthymius Zigabenus, early 12th century, Byzantine theologian, monk, and biblical commentator, 90

Eve, in Bible, the first woman and spouse of **Adam;** together they ate forbidden fruit in the Garden of Eden, 5, 49, 90

Ferdinand V, "the Catholic," 1452–1516, king of Sicily, Castile, and Aragon, who organized the Spanish Inquisition, 64

Festus, late 1st century, an assistant to the Roman Emperor **Domitian,** 19

Firmianus, see **Lactantius Firmianus**

Francis of Assisi, real name Giovanni Francesco Bernardone, 1182–1226, Italian preacher, miracle-worker, and founder of the Order of Friars Minor, 51, 55

Francisco de Vitoria, 1480?–1546, Spanish Dominican authority on the laws of war and a commentator on the writings of **Thomas Aquinas,** 53, 59, 87, 93

Galatino, Pietro Colonna, died 1539, Italian Franciscan theologian and historian of early Christianity, 40

Gelasius I, died 496, ecclesiastical statesman and pope during the reign of the Gothic King **Theodoric,** 34

Gentili, Alberico, 1552–1608, Italian jurist and early expert on international law who from 1581 taught at Oxford, 35

Georgius or **Zorzi, Francesco,** born 1460, Venetian writer influenced by Platonic mysticism and hermetic philosophy (see Rudick and Battin, p. 271), 88

Germanicus, died 157?, a young Christian of Smyrna who (in the story about Polycarp's martyrdom) aided the beast that killed him, 25

Gerson, Jean de, 1362?–1412, French theologian who favored church unity and ecclesiastical reforms, 52

Gorionides or **ben Gorion,** see **Yosippon**

Gratian, 359–383, Roman emperor who was defeated in Gaul by **Maximus,** 21

Gratian, 12th century, founder of the study of canon law, 34, 35–36, 40, 41, 42

Gregorio de Valencia, see **Valencia, Gregorio de**

Gregory the Great, 540–604, Roman nobleman who became bishop of Rome and reorganized church administration, claiming supremacy over all churches in Europe, 4, 36, 37, 71, 75

Gregory XII, real name Angelo Corrario or Correr, 1327–1417, the pope elected in 1406 by the Roman cardinals who were opposed to the pope at Avignon; Gregory resigned in 1415, 44

Gymnosophists, known to Europeans after 4th century BCE, Indian nudist philosophers who renounced bodily pleasures in order to devote themselves to meditation; a nonhereditary group were called **Samanaians,** 20

Hadrian, 76–138, Roman emperor who established far-flung boundaries of the Empire and built a wall across northern Britain, 26, 33

Hannibal, 247–183 BCE, Carthaginian general in Spain who conquered Rome, 19

Henry III, 1207–1272, king of England, son of **John Lackland**, 38

Herbert, Philip, 1584–1650, fourth earl of Pembroke and lord chamberlain to whom the first printed edition of *Biathanatos* was dedicated, 1

Hercules, in Greek mythology, a hero of extraordinary strength, 87

Herennius the Sicilian or Herennius Siculus, according to Valerius Maximus, a man of resolution and courage who killed himself by beating his head against a door-jamb, 19

Hermes, see **Tresmegistus, Hermes**

Herod the Great, 73?–4 BCE, the king of Judea at the time of the birth of **Jesus**, 23, 26, 62

Heron, early 4th century, according to **Cassian**, an aged hermit monk who attempted suicide, 61

Hieronymus, see **Jerome**

Hippocrates, 460?–?377 BCE, Greek physician who is called the father of medicine, 96

Hipponax, flourished 540–537 BCE, Greek iambic poet of Ephesus, famous for vituperative verse, some of which he wrote against a sculptor named **Bupalus**, 19

Homer, flourished as early as 1200 or as late as 850 BCE, ancient Greek poet to whom are attributed the *Iliad* and *Odyssey*, 19

Iamblichus, died 330?, Syrian neo-Platonist and pupil of Porphyry, 41

Ignatius of Antioch, early 2nd century, bishop of the church in Antioch who sought martyrdom under the Emperor Trajan; a Father of the church, 24, 25, 39, 62

Irenaeus, flourished late 2nd century, Christian bishop in Gaul and a Father of the church, said to have been martyred under the Emperor Septimius Severus, 86

Isidore of Seville, 560?–636, archbishop of Seville and a Father of the church who was considered the most learned person of his time, 11

Isidorus, 1st century BCE, a contemporary of Augustus who held many slaves, 38

Jacob, also called Israel, in Bible, a Hebrew patriarch and the son of Isaac and twin of Esau, father of the twelve founders of the tribes of Israel, 86

Jephthah, in Bible, an early Hebrew judge who sacrficed to Jahweh his only daughter in fulfillment of a vow, 90

Jeremiah, 650?–?585 BCE, a major Hebrew prophet of the Deuteronomic period, 14

Jerome, real name Eusebius Hieronymus, 340?–420, Latin biblical scholar and a Father of the church, 4, 5, 12, 23, 35, 37, 39, 41–43, 53–54, 55, 71, 84, 88, 97

Jesuits, 1540–, members of the Roman Catholic Society of Jesus, founded by Ignatius Loyola, 3, 28, 41, 56, 59, 83

Jesus of Nazareth, 4? BCE–?29 CE, founder of Christianity who accepted sentencing as a blasphemer to be executed by crucifixion, 22, 33, 43, 54, 55, 57, 71, 73–74, 77, 81–85, 87, 89, 91

Job, in Bible, a Hebrew patriarch who suffered vicissitudes as tests sent by God, 8, 70–72

John the Baptist, 1st century, in New Testament, the son of Zacharias and Elizabeth who baptized his cousin **Jesus**, 23, 55

John the Evangelist, 1st century, author of the fourth gospel, 90

John Lackland, 1167?–1216, king of England who swore fealty to Pope Innocent III and was forced by his barons to sign the Magna Charta, 58

John XXII, real name **Jacques d'Euse**, 1249–1334, pope from 1316, 44

Lucidus, late 5th century, author of a letter to thirty bishops who accused him of heresy, whose defense was that some Christians were saved by the law of nature (see Rudick and Battin, pp. 212–13), 14, 20

Lucrecia, Roman woman who, according to Livy and Ovid, killed herself after being raped (see Rudick and Battin, p. 274), 92

Lyra, see **Nicholas of Lyra**

Macer, see **Licinius Macer, Gaius**

Macrobius, Ambrosius Theodosius, 5th century, Latin neo-Platonic author, 45

Maldonado, Juan, 1553–1583, Spanish **Jesuit** theologian and biblical scholar, 52

Malloni, Daniel, flourished early 16th century, Brescia-born public teacher of scriptures in Bologna, 82, 89

Manichaeans, from 2nd century onwards into Middle Ages, adherents of a dualistic, ascetical religion, influential upon **Elkesai** and **Augustine,** 76

Marcellina, 4th century, sister of **Ambrose of Milan,** 63

Mariana, Juan de, 1536–1623 or 1624, Spanish **Jesuit** theologian who advocated regicide on religious grounds, 56, 59

Mark, John, 1st century, in New Testament, with **Paul** and **Barnabas** a missionary worker, traditionally regarded as author of the second Christian gospel, 56

Marlorat, Augustin, 1506–1562, French Reformed biblical scholar and defender of the Huguenots, 79, 83

Martyr, Peter, see **Peter Martyr**

Mary, Virgin, 1st century, in New Testament, the mother of **Jesus,** 76, 82

Matthew, late 1st century, the name of the person to whom is attributed the first book of the New Testament, 55

Maximian, died 310, Roman emperor who conspired against **Constantine I** and committed suicide, 25

Maximus, Magnus Clemens, died 388, Spanish-born Roman emperor who led an insurrection in Britain and defeated the Emperor **Gratian** in Gaul; see also **Paulus Maximus,** 21

Mazzolini, Sylvester, 1460–1523, Italian Dominican theologian, prolific writer, and author of *Summa summarium,* 50, 83

Meirus son of Belgas, died 70, according to the historian **Josephus,** a man who with **Joseph son of Dalaeus** threw himself into the flames as the Romans burned the Temple in Jerusalem, 25

Menghi, Girolamo, died 1610, Italian demonologist and exorcist, 61

Miletus, Virgins of, maidens in that ancient Greek city who customarily hanged themselves; when a decree required that their bodies be borne naked to their graves, they desisted (according to the *Attic Nights* by Aulus Gellius, who got it from Plutarch), 40

Molther, Johann, 1561–1618, a German anti-Jewish theologian, 40

Montanists, 2nd century, spiritualist Christians, originating in Phrygia, who prophesied the end of the world, 55

More, Thomas, 1478–1535, English scholar and vice-chancellor who was executed under King Henry VIII, 29, 51

Moses, possibly 1200 BCE, in Bible, Israelite leader of the exodus from Egypt and the Israelites' and Jews' lawgiver, 21, 55, 69, 76, 77, 85, 95

Paracelsus, Philippus Aureolus, real name Theophrastus Bombastus von Hohenheim, 1493?–1541, Swiss alchemist and physician, 75, 95, 96

Parentucelli, see **Nicholas V**

Paul of Burgos, 1351?–1435, Spanish rabbi who converted to Christianity through studying scriptures and **Aquinas** and who became bishop of Cartagena and later of Burgos, 89, 93

Paul of Tarsus, died 65?, a Pharisaic Jew who converted to Christianity and became its main early missionary and the earliest known Christian writer, 13, 14, 15, 51, 71, 74–78, 80–82, 84–85

Paulinus of Nola, 353–431, French Christian who became a bishop in Italy and practiced strict asceticism, 10, 24, 43, 56, 61, 85, 88

Paulus Maximus, 16th century, a youth visited by **Philip Neri,** 51

Pedraza, Juan de, 16th century, Spanish moral theologian and author of sacramental dramas, 64, 88

Pelagia of Antioch, died 304?, a fifteen-year-old Christian who took her life when soldiers came to seize and to violate her, 63

Pereira, Benito, 1535?–1610, Spanish **Jesuit** biblical scholar who taught at Rome and wrote on magic and superstition, 29, 88

Peter, died 65?, in New Testament, a leading apostle of **Jesus** who by tradition was martyred in Rome, 55, 82

Peter Comestor, died 1179?, French biblical scholar and author of *Scholastic History,* recounting events from the creation to the death of **Paul of Tarsus,** 88

Peter the Lombard, 1100?–1160, Italian-born scholastic theologian, famous for his *Book of Sentences,* 10, 80

Peter Martyr, real name Pietro Martire Vermigli, 1500–1562, Florentine Augustininan monk and Protestant reformer who taught at Strassburg, Oxford, and Zürich, 42–43, 50, 51, 64, 79

Petilianus, early 5th century, a Donatist bishop against whom **Augustine** wrote, 27, 91

Petronius, see **Arbiter, Gaius Petronius**

Pharisees, from 2nd century BCE, a Jewish religious party prominent from the time of the Maccabean wars until the fall of Jerusalem, 80

Pico della Mirandola, Giovanni, 1463–1494, Florentine Renaissance scholar and Platonist, 18, 76

Pilate, Pontius, 1st century, Roman procurator of Palestine who sentenced **Jesus** to crucifixion, 82

Pindar, 522?–443 BCE, Greek lyric poet, 42

Plato, 427–347 BCE, Greek philosopher, a disciple of **Socrates** and teacher of **Aristotle,** 22, 29, 51, 92, 97

Pliny the Elder, 23–79, Roman scholar and writer, 6, 10, 38, 64

Pollio, see **Vedius Pollio, Publius**

Pomponazzi, Pietro, 1462–1525, Italian anti-Thomist philosopher and humanist, 96

Porcia, died 42 BCE, daughter of Cato of Utica, wife of Bibulus and then of the Brutus who assassinated **Julius Caesar,** 19

Porcius Latro, Marcus, 53 BCE?–?4 CE, Spanish-born Augustan rhetor and close friend of the elder Seneca, 19

Prester John, legendary medieval ruler of an oriental Christian kingdom, 55

Priscus, see **Tarquinius Priscus, Lucius**

Solomon, died 933? BCE, in Bible, son of David and Bathsheba who became king of
Israel and built the Temple in Jerusalem, 4, 6, 69

Solon, 639?–?559 BCE, Athenian lawgiver and advocate of moderate democracy, 39

Soto, Dominic, 1494–1560, Spanish-born Dominican theologian, 12, 41, 45, 52, 53–
54, 59, 73, 93

Stephen V, flourished 885–891, pope whose election was rejected by King Charles
the Fat, 58

Sulpicius Severus, 360?–?410, Gallic Christian ascetic, historian, and biographer of
Martin of Tours, 43, 49

Sylvius, Antonius Clarus, published 1603, author of commentary on civil, canon,
and Roman law, 13, 21

Tabbai, Judah ben, a rabbi and Mishnaic sage cited by Serarius and from him by
Donne, 4

Tacitus, Cornelius, 55?–after 117, Roman orator, rhetorician, and historian, 20

Tarquinius Priscus, Lucius, flourished 616–578 BCE, fifth of the legendary kings of
the early Romans, 40

Terence, 190?–?159 BCE, Roman playwright of Latin comedies, 19

Tertullian, Quintus Septimius, 160?–?225, Latin Christian writer in North Africa
and extoller of martyrdom, 3, 22, 23, 27

Theodoric the Great, 454?–526, king of the Ostrogoths who ruled Italy from
Ravenna, 34, 44

Theodosius I, 346?–395, Roman general and emperor in Constantinople who
required that citizens be orthodox Christians, 21, 41

Theophylact, 11th century, Byzantine biblical commentator, 90

Thyraeus, Peter, early 17th century, German Jesuit theologian and demonologist,
42–43

Toledo, Francisco de, 1532–1596, Spanish Jesuit theologian and the first Jesuit to
be named a cardinal, 51, 54, 56, 57

Torres, Francisco de, 1509–1584 or 1586, Spanish Jesuit casuist, patristic scholar,
and controversialist against various Protestants, especially Lutherans, 55

Trajan, 52 or 53–117, Spanish-born Roman emperor, 10, 64

Trent, Council of, 1545–1563, meetings of Roman Catholic leaders in reaction to
Protestant Reformation and the main agency of the Counter-Reformation, 71

Tresmegistus, Hermes, early CE, purported author of Greek and Latin mystical
writings known as the Hermetic books, 5

Ursperg, see Konrad of Lichtenau

Usuard, 9th century, French monk and priest who wrote stories of martyrs, 63

Valencia, Gregorio de, 1549–1603, Spanish Jesuit theologian and commentator on
writings by Aquinas, 87, 93

Valens, 328?–378, Roman emperor in Constantinople, 25, 41

Vandals, 5th century, a Germanic people from the Baltic region who at this time
overran western Europe and North Africa, 56

Vázquez, Gabriel, 1549–1604, Spanish Jesuit theologian who taught mainly at
Alcalá, 28, 61

Vedius Pollio, Publius, died 19 BCE, minister of Augustus, a notorious horseman
who fed slaves to the lampreys in his Camanian villa, 38